Why Study Colossians?

I slowly began to slide down in my seat at the dinner table as the dreaded topic of discussion came up. Oh, you know the one. The family member speaking had strong opinions on the matter. Most everyone around the table nodded their heads in agreement. However, I had literally just come off the heels of another family gathering — a gathering that also had strong opinions, but opinions of the other side. It struck me as odd ... how could these people, all of whom I love so dearly, have such different opinions? Even more curious, how could these wonderful, loving, kind, Jesus-loving Christians be on total opposite sides? And as someone stuck in the middle, how was I to know which side was right?!

All that to say, this guide will completely debunk the myth that there can somehow be "your truth" and "my truth." Colossians 1:5 says the *"word of the truth"* is *"the gospel."* The gospel of Jesus Christ is our standard for truth. It is the only Truth that we live and die for. And truthfully, the gospel is enough. The gospel is sufficient for all of our troubles, worries and needs. But is it sufficient for our divided opinions?

Paul's letter to the Colossians addressed a church that felt like they were in the middle of a tug-of-war match. On one side was the fresh idolatry of Rome attempting to creep into Christianity. On the other side was the Jewish community insisting on its old ways. But what Rome and Judaism had in common was telling new Christians that Jesus wasn't the answer — at least, not the full answer.

None of us are too far removed from this situation. We have so many competing voices telling us what to believe. And when we do go to the Word of Truth, it is difficult not to read the gospel through our own lenses, looking for what we want to see. Differences occur among us. Strong opinions develop, and divides crack the ground between us. And I'm not pointing fingers. As I once heard said, "If you think you are the 'Jesus' in this situation, you are not." None of us are perfect.

The only place we can find Truth is in Jesus Christ. So with Colossians as our guide, we will spend the next five weeks looking at Jesus. Let's block the noise, the opinions and the divisions and focus on the only Truth that will never fail us. We will make imperfect progress, but it will still be progress! And maybe, just maybe, we will come away realizing we have a Truth that unites us, differing opinions and all.

colossians

Letter to Colossians: The Writer

The New Testament book of Colossians is what we refer to as an epistle. This simply means it is a letter. Let's take a moment to look at who wrote this letter.

Formal letters would begin with the name of the sender. Colossians 1:1 starts out with *"Paul, an apostle of Christ Jesus by the will of God, and Timothy our brother."* Oftentimes a letter would be dictated while a secretary or assistant transcribed the words. This is what we believe took place with Colossians. Paul dictated while Timothy transcribed. The letter of Colossians appears to have been written at the same time as Philemon and Ephesians, as these all were delivered by the same person. (Ephesians 6:21; Colossians 4:7) This places the letters around A.D. 62, meaning Paul would have been imprisoned in Rome during this time. Paul used his time in prison to continue sharing, spreading and strengthening the gospel Truth.

Since we live in a world of divided opinions today, it is important to point out that Paul was quite familiar with such a world. On one side, he had his fellow Jewish population, many of whom felt threatened by Jesus and His teachings. On the other side were Paul's fellow Roman citizens, who didn't know what to make of Christians and their different way of living. Even within the new, growing body of Christians, Paul experienced divided opinions! Paul had disagreements with the Apostle Peter on several occasions, specifically over gentile inclusion. One noteworthy disagreement Paul had was with his friend and ministry partner, Barnabas. On their missionary journey together, they had brought along a man named John Mark. From this point forward, we'll refer to him as "Mark" since this is the name by which he is more commonly known. Somewhere along the way, Mark bailed out. When it came time for a second missionary journey, Barnabas wanted to take Mark again; Paul did not. Neither was right or wrong; they just had different opinions that ended with the two men going different ways. Yet what is so fascinating is that here in the letter of Colossians, years after this event took place, we see Mark's name mentioned again, this time as a friend and fellow worker with Paul. (Colossians 4:10) What happened? Had Paul's opinion of Mark changed? Or had Mark changed? Perhaps both. Either way, we can learn from the life of Paul that differing opinions are a normal part of relationships, both outside and inside the Church.

But there was one thing that Paul never wavered on, and that was the Truth. In Colossians, Paul said that *"Christ is all"* (Colossians 3:11). There is only one gospel, only one Truth, and that is Jesus Christ. In 2 Corinthians 10:5, Paul says, *"We destroy arguments and every lofty opinion raised against the knowledge of God, and take every thought captive to obey Christ."* No other argument or opinion matters, only the truth of Christ. Paul also believed in speaking this truth *"in love"* (Ephesians 4:15). This meant patience and kindness, not envy or boasting, not arrogance or rudeness, not irritability or resentfulness, not even insistence on one's own way! (1 Corinthians 13:4-5) Paul believed in the power of God to reveal the truth. He knew his job was only to share Truth. If a person still thought differently than him, he left it in God's hands. (Philippians 3:15)

Paul was no stranger to the shifting sands of dividing opinions. But he also knew his feet were planted on the solid foundation of Truth, which is Jesus Christ.

IN WHAT WAY IS IT REASSURING TO LEARN THAT THE EARLY CHURCH ALSO LIVED IN A WORLD OF DIVIDED OPINIONS, YET THE TRUTH OF CHRIST STILL STANDS TODAY?

colossians

Letter to Colossians: The Recipient

During the times of Paul, letters followed a standard style. As we've mentioned, the first line was the name of the sender. The second line was the name of the intended recipient. Colossians 1:2 says, *"To the saints and faithful brothers in Christ at Colossae."* Let's take a look at the church in Colossae.

The ancient city of Colossae was located in modern-day Turkey — although today the city is nothing more than an unexcavated mound. It was located a little more than 100 miles to the east of Ephesus in what was known as the Lycus River valley. At the height of its existence, Colossae prospered as a city on the trade route linking the Aegean Sea and the Euphrates River. It was well known for its textile industry, particularly a distinctive, glossy, deep-purple wool. This location also made Colossae a region diverse in ethnicity, religion and culture.

By the time Paul began his missionary journeys, the trade route had changed, leaving Colossae off the beaten path. While still a large city, it was surpassed in importance by the neighboring cities of Laodicea and Hierapolis. Also, history tells us that near the time Paul wrote this letter to Colossae (around A.D. 61-63), a massive earthquake struck the city, leaving it devastated. There was an attempt to rebuild, but as time marched on, the city did not. It was eventually abandoned at some point during the Middle Ages.

It is interesting to note that Paul seems to have never visited the city of Colossae. The church of the Colossians appears to have been planted by a man named Epaphras. (Colossians 1:7) Most scholars agree that Epaphras was likely converted to Christianity by Paul while he was in Ephesus. Epaphras then returned to his hometown of Colossae to share the Good News, which he also spread to Laodicea and Hierapolis. Epaphras later went to visit Paul in prison and told him about the condition of the Colossian church. (Colossians 1:8-9) This visit is what prompted the Apostle Paul to write the letter we are studying today.

Paul was concerned about Epaphras' report. It seems there was someone (or a group of someones) who was spreading false teaching through the young church in Colossae. Scholars have different suggestions as to what this teaching was. Some say perhaps the false teaching was a pagan cult, but others say legalistic Judaism, and still others suggest an early form of Gnosticism — a complex belief system that emphasized special knowledge, often obtained through astrology or magic. The Gnostics believed salvation came by this special knowledge, not by faith. Gnostics also believed all matter was evil; therefore, God in Christ could never take a human body. Under this idea, Christ was either not divine or not human. All of these ideas were a dangerous untruth. The problems facing Colossae could have been a mix of all of the above. [1] What we do know is that these false teachings were undermining the complete and superior authority of Jesus Christ. Paul wanted to make clear that Christ is the Truth.

Today we can use the letter of Colossians to also make clear to us the Truth. Christ is *"before all things, and in him all things hold together"* (Colossians 1:17). If we want to know the Truth, we look to Jesus Christ.

WHAT ARE SOME WAYS YOU HAVE LEARNED TO RECOGNIZE UNTRUTH? HOW DO YOU GUARD AGAINST UNTRUTH?

Colossians' Connection to Philemon

Closely associated with the book of Colossians is a tiny book of the Bible called Philemon. Philemon is also an epistle (letter). It is only one chapter long, written to one specific man. What exactly do we know about Philemon, and how does he relate to Colossians? Let's compare the two.

The letters of Colossians and Philemon were both sent from *"Paul ... and Timothy"* (Philemon 1:1). They were written near the same time and both were sent with Tychicus and Onesimus. They share many of the same names and references. (Colossians 4:7-17; Philemon 1:2, 23-24) The two books also share a personal connection. The story goes like this:

▶ The church of Colossae met in the home of a man named Philemon. (Philemon 1:1-2)

▶ Philemon had a bondservant named Onesimus, but Onesimus had fled to Rome and possibly had stolen money or property from Philemon. Onesimus was then a fugitive.

▶ Somehow, in Rome, Onesimus came across a man named Paul who taught him about Jesus Christ. He became a Christian and became a great help to Paul in prison.

▶ Paul knew Onesimus needed to address his past, so he sent him back to Colossae — back to his master, Philemon — with letters for both the Colossian church and specifically for Philemon, encouraging him to receive Onesimus back as *"a beloved brother"* (Philemon 1:16). Paul was so convinced of Jesus' work in Onesimus' life that he even offered to personally pay off anything owed. Perhaps Paul was also so convinced of Jesus' work in Philemon's life that he knew he wouldn't have to pay. Paul said, *"Confident of your obedience, I write to you, knowing that you will do even more than I say"* (Philemon 1:21).

How touching to see not only Paul's concern for the Church as a whole but also his specific concern for individual people. The gospel of Christ is not just for the "world." It is for the person standing next to you in line. It is for your neighbor, your co-worker, your friend.

WHO SPECIFICALLY CAN YOU ENCOURAGE AND LOVE TODAY IN THE NAME OF JESUS?

What You Have To Look Forward to in This Colossians Study Guide

In addition to the background information and daily questions for studying Colossians, we have also included several elements to deepen your study along the way.

TRUTH IN ART

Often we think of truth in terms of cold, hard facts. However, our Creator God has infused imagination, innovation and inspiration into this world that we might see the Truth in this way as well. Truth can be found in a song, a painting, a dance, a quilt. We were designed to perceive Truth in artistic forms as well. In this study guide, we look at a few truths through the lens of art.

▶ **Hymns of the New Testament:** It turns out one of the first Christian hymns just may be found here in Colossians.
▶ We also created artwork inspired by the book of Colossians for you to enjoy, including:

   "Rooted" from Colossians 2:6-7.

   "Old Self vs. New Self" from Colossians 3:1-17.
▶ You might even find a couple of places within the daily questions where you can try your hand at a little artistic expression as well.

PRAYING COLOSSIANS

A powerful "extra" that we have added to this study guide is a daily prayer prompt to guide you through praying the scriptures of Colossians. There is so much benefit in using the Bible to direct our prayers. Turning each verse into a prayer provides us with fresh words and thoughts. We have specifics from the Word to pray over our family, our friends, our communities and ourselves. This also helps us to focus during our time of prayer. (Surely I am not the only one who struggles here!) But perhaps most important to this study, praying the Scripture is praying Truth. We can have complete confidence when we pray Scripture that we are praying in accordance to God's will and Word. These prayer prompts found at the end of each day will help teach us how to pray the Word of God during our study time.

WEEKEND MATCH-UPS

At the end of each week, we'll compare two different concepts. At times, we may think one of these beliefs is a little more important than the other. (For example, should we express more truth or more grace?) Other times, the two ideas might look like completely opposing opinions. Our goal is to take both sides and simply allow the Bible to reveal the truth. You will have an opportunity to write down what you learn and to brainstorm ideas to apply that truth for the week. Our Weekend Match-Ups include:

Truth vs. Grace

Condemnation vs. Conviction

Worldly Wisdom vs. Spiritual Wisdom

Humility, Meekness, Submission and Servanthood vs. Modern Society

My Personal Relationship With Jesus vs. My Relationship With the Church

APPLYING THE WORD TODAY

To take our two main ideas for this study ("knowing the Truth" and "divided opinions") just another step further, we have two additional sections to help us apply the Word to our lives today. These two sections include:

How To Spot (and Stop) False Teachings

The Great Divides

IN CASE YOU WERE WONDERING

Wrapping up our study guide, you will find 10 verses from Colossians that maybe you have heard somewhere before. Our First 5 team has written a quick study on each verse to take you even deeper into the meaning, context or Greek origins. This is your chance to get into the fun details of Scripture and have an even richer understanding and appreciation of God's Word the next time you hear a verse used.

WHICH OF THESE CONTENT FEATURES ARE YOU MOST LOOKING FORWARD TO?

colossians

THE OVERLAP OF ALL FOUR MISSIONARY JOURNEYS

This map shows Paul's four major missionary journeys. The map highlights that Paul traveled around and near Colossae, but likely never visited there. While Paul's exact routes cannot be determined, these routes are based on the evidence we have in Scripture as well as historical evidence for known travel routes.

Italy

ROME●

Black Sea

Macedonia

PHILIPPI●

THESSALONICA●

Achaia

CORINTH●

Crete

Asia

EPHESUS●

LAODICEA●

COLOSSAE●

Galatia

ANTIOCH●

Cyprus

Syria

CAESAREA●

Palestine

JERUSALEM●

Mediterranean Sea

Major Moments

WEEK 1

Colossians 1:1-2 | Paul (an apostle of Jesus) and Timothy wrote to the church of Colossae.
Colossians 1:3-5a | Indicators of a Christ-follower are faith, love and hope.
Colossians 1:5b-8 | The gospel is the word of Truth.
Colossians 1:9-10a | Paul prayed that Christians would be filled with knowledge and spiritual wisdom.
Colossians 1:10b-14 | Walking with Christ bears fruit, gives us endurance and results in thanksgiving.

WEEK 2

Colossians 1:15-17 | Christ is before all things.
Colossians 1:18-20 | Christ is preeminent.
Colossians 1:21-23 | Once hostile, we are now reconciled.
Colossians 1:24-29 | We rejoice in suffering and mature in Christ.
Colossians 2:1-5 | In Christ, we find wisdom and knowledge.

WEEK 3

Colossians 2:6-7 | We are rooted in Christ.
Colossians 2:8-10 | Empty, deceitful philosophies can lead us astray.
Colossians 2:11-15 | We were dead in sin but are made alive in Christ.
Colossians 2:16-19 | Let no one judge or disqualify you, but hold fast to Christ.
Colossians 2:20-23 | Beware of human teachings that appear religious but have no value.

WEEK 4

Colossians 3:1-4 | Our life is Christ.
Colossians 3:5-11 | We put to death what is earthly in us.
Colossians 3:12-15 | We put on virtues of Christ.
Colossians 3:16-17 | We do everything in the name of Jesus.
Colossians 3:18-4:1 | Let's look like Christ in our homes.

WEEK 5

Colossians 4:2-4 | Continue steadfastly in prayer.
Colossians 4:5-6 | Walk in wisdom and talk with seasoning.
Colossians 4:7-9 | Both veteran ministers and new converts can spread the gospel.
Colossians 4:10-14 | The Church is filled with individual, unique people who work together for Christ.
Colossians 4:15-18 | The Church is one big family.

Week
One

Colossians 1:1–2

PAUL (AN APOSTLE OF JESUS) AND TIMOTHY
WROTE TO THE CHURCH OF COLOSSAE.

The letter of Colossians opens with the typical letterhead greeting of the time. The greeting first tells us the sender, followed by the intended receiver. Let's take a look at both.

According to Colossians 1:1, who are the two senders of this letter, and what titles or qualifications follow their names?

Paul – apostle of Christ Jesus by God's will
Timothy – our brother

The term "apostle" referred to someone the risen Christ called and commissioned. And Paul says this term applied to him *"by the will of God"* (Colossians 1:1). This is important because it gives this letter a different level of authority. During the days of the early Christian Church, as these letters and accounts were being copied, shared and gathered together to eventually form what we know as our New Testament, a letter known to be sent from the Apostle Paul would have been unquestionably added to the canon (which is a fancy word that refers to the exact collection of works that make up our Bibles). Because Paul was an apostle of Jesus, by the will of God, we believe the words he wrote to be inspired by the Holy Spirit and truly the words of God.

Read Peter's words in 2 Peter 3:15-16. Peter compared Paul's letters (and some people's tendency to misunderstand or twist them) to the other _____. Meaning Peter believed Paul's letters to be considered what? (Hint: It's the same word.)

What does 2 Timothy 3:16 say about the origin of Scripture?

It is inspired by God

In this study, we will talk about how to know the Truth. It is important to know where Truth comes from. It doesn't come from the majority. It doesn't come from "within ourselves." Truth, by definition, needs a standard, a reality.

According to Jesus' prayer in John 17:17, what is Truth?

God's Word

Next, let's look at the original receiver of this letter.

Colossians 1:2 says it was written to the saints and faithful brothers in Christ located where? *Colossae*

The church of Colossae was filled with a mix of Jewish and gentile converts. Each person came with their own background, their own worldview and their own unique experiences. For the first time in history, these people were working to unite together under Christ. And contending with the church on the outside was the indulgent, superstitious, extravagant worship of whichever Roman deity you chose, as well as the tradition-soaked, law-filled worship of the Jewish community. Talk about a world of divided opinions!

Where do you see divisions in the world today? Do any of these affect you directly?

— Political
— medical
— Religious

When you think about divided opinions, what words or phrases come to your mind to describe that atmosphere?

- tension filled
- division
- heated
- judgment

I think of words like "conflict" or "judgment." However, what two words does Paul use in Colossians 1:2 to greet the church and set the tone?

* Grace to you *
* Peace from God our father

How might these two words make a difference in our world of divided opinions as well?

- might not escalate to the point where relationships end
- possibly help keep our tempers in check

Praying Colossians 1:1–2

THANK GOD FOR THE GIFT OF HIS WORD AND HIS TRUTH.
PRAY FOR GRACE AND PEACE OVER YOUR HOME, WORKPLACE,
CHURCH AND CITY.

Colossians 1:3–5a

INDICATORS OF A CHRIST-FOLLOWER ARE FAITH, LOVE AND HOPE.

Today's reading begins with the mention of prayer. Paul prayed for the Christians in Colossae. However, what is interesting is that Paul likely never traveled to Colossae. He did not know this group personally. But this did not stop him from praying for them.

How often in your own prayers do you pray for someone or some group that you do not know personally? *not much*

In verses 4-5a, we come across what are sometimes known as the three pillars of "theological virtues." These are three principles that define the Christian life.

Fill in the words for Colossians 1:4-5a (we will use the ESV translation).

"...since we heard of your **faith** *in Christ Jesus and of the* **love** *that you have for all the saints, because of the* **hope** *laid up for you in heaven."*

What three words are mentioned in 1 Corinthians 13:13?

faith, hope + love

I like Pastor Charles Swindoll's description of these three pillars in his commentary *Living Insights.* He says, "Faith **looks back** to the anchor of salvation — Jesus Christ's person and work. Love **looks around,** building up the body of Christ through selfless service toward one another ... Hope **looks ahead** to the unalterable promise of God the Father, that He will one day usher us into His presence" [1] (emphasis added).

Use the space below to draw some kind of representation of faith, love and hope in your life. Do not worry if you are not a great artist. The idea is simply to create a visual that will help you remember this biblical truth.

Why might these three principles be foundational to Christianity?

Praying Colossians 1:3–5a
TAKE A MOMENT TO PRAY FOR SOMEONE YOU HAVE NEVER PERSONALLY MET. THANK GOD FOR THEM. ALSO PRAY FOR OTHERS IN YOUR LIFE, BY NAME, TO GROW IN THEIR FAITH IN CHRIST, IN THEIR LOVE FOR OTHERS AND IN THEIR HOPE FOR HEAVEN. FINALLY, PRAY THE SAME FOR YOUR OWN HEART.

colossians

Colossians 1

THE GOSPEL IS THE WORD

Before we begin today, let's take a quick moment to review

According to Jesus' prayer in John 17:17, what is Truth:

Now fill in the blanks for Colossians 1:5b.

"Of this you have heard before in the _____ of the truth, the _____,"

What does this teach us about truth?

The gospel of Jesus Christ is Truth. Listen to how New Testament scholar N.T. Wright describes it: "[The gospel] is not, primarily, either an invitation or a technique for changing people's lives. It is a command to be obeyed and a power let loose in the world." [1] In other words, the gospel of Jesus Christ isn't a suggestion or an opinion. It isn't one of many ideas we might choose from. The gospel of Jesus is the Truth.

...e down Jesus' words from John 14:6.

We live in a time of divided opinions. The world says you can have "your truth" and I can have "mine." What does today's passage teach us about truth?

Often when I think of my spiritual journey, I think of it in terms of how "I came to Christ." However, Colossians 1:6 uses very different language. It says that the gospel of Christ *"has come to you."*

Do you also think in terms of you coming to Christ? In what ways have Christ and the gospel come to you?

The gospel of Christ is so much bigger than just us. Verse 6 says it has come to *"the whole world."* In the times of the Old Testament, the plan of God was tied to the line of Abraham. Now, under Jesus, that plan has been unleashed into all the world. In the whole world, it is *"bearing fruit and increasing"* (Colossians 1:6). The truth of Jesus transcends nationalities, cultural differences and differing worldviews.

How does seeing the gospel at work throughout the whole world strengthen and confirm your belief in Jesus?

While we have learned that the gospel is Truth and that this Truth comes to us, let's talk for a moment about **how** it comes to us. Romans 10:14c says, *"And how are they to hear without someone preaching?"* God often uses His faithful followers to spread the Truth to others.

According to Colossians 1:7, who taught the church in Colossae about Christ? What do we learn about him from this verse?

Who was instrumental in your life to teach you the truth of Christ?

Praying Colossians 1:5b–8

PRAY FOR THE GOSPEL OF TRUTH TO BE UNLEASHED IN THE WHOLE WORLD. PRAY FOR IT TO COME TO SPECIFIC PEOPLE BY NAME. PRAY FOR GOD TO SEND THEM AN EPAPHRAS. PRAY THAT MORE OF US WOULD RISE UP TO BE AN EPAPHRAS FOR SOMEONE ELSE.

colossians

Colossians 1:9–10a

PAUL PRAYED THAT CHRISTIANS WOULD BE
FILLED WITH KNOWLEDGE AND SPIRITUAL WISDOM.

Today's reading starts with the words *"And so ..."* (Colossians 1:9). This means the following sentence needs to be understood with the previous comments in mind. Previously, Paul mentioned how he and Timothy *"heard of"* the Colossians' faith (v. 4) and love (v. 8). Once again, Paul mentions in verse 9 about the *"day we heard."*

All of this information they had heard caused Paul and Timothy to do what, according to the next part of verse 9?

This was a particularly dear theme for Paul throughout all of his letters. This is also a vital part of our journey through this study guide as we learn how to know and apply Truth. Fill in the chart below with each verse's thoughts on prayer.

ROMANS 12:12	
1 THESSALONIANS 5:17	
PHILIPPIANS 4:6	
EPHESIANS 6:18	
COLOSSIANS 4:2	

Very purposefully, Paul prays that the church of Colossae would be filled with "gnosis," or knowledge.

According to Colossians 1:9, what kind of knowledge is this specifically?

Read 2 Peter 3:18. What is the best knowledge to grow in?

Knowledge itself isn't the final destination. In fact, knowledge alone can be very dangerous.

What warning is given in 1 Corinthians 8:1?

"Puffs up" implies pride (the bad kind) where you think more highly of yourself than you ought. Love "builds up" or strengthens others and the Church. Take a moment to examine your own life. Is your search for knowledge tempered with love? How do you know? And why should we not separate knowledge from love?

Seventeenth-century author and theologian Matthew Henry once said, "We must know it, in order to do it." [1] Knowledge of the truth should lead us toward action. It needs to be applied.

Colossians 1:10a says to be filled with knowledge and spiritual wisdom, *"so as to"* what?

Tomorrow we will talk specifically about what this looks like, but to end today, how would you describe your "walk"? How might others from the outside describe it? Does it reflect spiritual wisdom? Why or why not?

Praying Colossians 1:9–10a

PRAY FOR THE ENDURANCE AND DISCIPLINE TO *"NOT [CEASE] TO PRAY."* PRAY FOR PEOPLE BY NAME, THAT THEY MAY BE *"FILLED WITH THE KNOWLEDGE OF [GOD'S] WILL"* (V. 9). PRAY THAT KNOWLEDGE WOULD BE TEMPERED WITH LOVE AND WOULD CHANGE HOW WE BEHAVE.

Colossians 1:10b–14

WALKING WITH CHRIST BEARS FRUIT,
GIVES US ENDURANCE AND RESULTS IN THANKSGIVING.

Yesterday we talked about our need for spiritual knowledge and wisdom. This knowledge results in action. Our good behavior does not save us (because none of us act good enough to merit salvation), but our salvation does fill us with a love and joy that encourages us to act more like Jesus. So how do we *"walk in a manner worthy of the Lord"* (v. 10)? That is our focus for today. We are going to look at it in three parts.

COLOSSIANS 1:10B – BEARING FRUIT

The first aspect we will notice of our new life in Christ is fruit. It is interesting that Paul uses the phrase *"bearing fruit."* This would have brought to mind the creation story, where God created and then told creation to go forth and multiply.

According to 2 Corinthians 5:17, in Christ, we are what?

As the new creation, we are to *"bear fruit."* What fruit should start to show in our walk with Christ, according to Galatians 5:22-23?

At the end of Colossians 1:10, we see repeated again the *"knowledge"* of God. This time it says *"increasing."* You might call this a spiral argument. [1] Knowledge will help us walk in a way that pleases God. And walking in holiness will actually help increase our knowledge. And around and around it will go, ever increasing. Take a moment to draw a spiral, starting with knowledge, then growing in your walk, increasing in knowledge, growing in your walk more... What does this mean to you?

The next aspect we will see in our walk with Christ is an increase in *"endurance and patience with joy."* Rarely do we talk about endurance and patience in the same sentence as the word "joy." Endurance and patience carry the idea of having the power to withstand hardship, stress, pain or unhappiness. [2]

Why might endurance and patience be especially important for a Christian living in a world of divided opinions?

This is hard. That is why it is so important to point out that we cannot do this in our own power. Rather, Colossians 1:11 says, *"being strengthened with all power, according to his glorious might, for all endurance and patience with joy"* (emphasis added). Whose power strengthens us to withstand?

According to 1 Corinthians 1:24, who is the power of God (**and**, interestingly, the wisdom of God)?

The final aspect we notice in the life of a Christ-follower is thankfulness. Gratitude is the natural result of walking with Jesus. Let's look at all we have to be thankful for just from these three verses:

What do each of these verses mean in your own words?
We have been qualified to *"share in the _____ of the saints in light"* (v. 12).

"He has _____ us _____ the domain of _____..." (v. 13). Praise God for this!

"...and transferred us to" what (v. 13)?

Above all, we can be eternally grateful because in Christ we have what, according to verse 14?

Praying Colossians 1:10b-14

TODAY, PRAY THAT GOD WOULD INCREASE YOUR KNOWLEDGE OF HIM, HELPING YOU WALK CLOSER TO HIM, THEREBY INCREASING YOUR KNOWLEDGE OF HIM. PRAY FOR THOSE WHO NEED GOD'S POWER FOR ENDURANCE AND PATIENCE TODAY. FINALLY, GIVE THANKS, TELLING GOD SPECIFICALLY WHAT YOU ARE THANKFUL FOR.

Weekend Reflections

We live in a divided world. Opinions are yelled at us from all sides. This can sometimes leave us feeling confused and asking, *What is the truth?* During our weekends on the study of Colossians, let's tackle some of these broader areas with the truth of God's Word.

For Week 1, read the section titled **"Truth vs. Grace"** on page 32.

Have you witnessed division in terms of truth and grace? Where specifically?

What do you learn about truth and grace from God's Word?

How can you walk in both of these this week?

Truth vs. Grace

One of the areas where we can see divided opinions is in regard to truth and grace. Often, depending on upbringing and personality, a person will tend to lean more one way than another. Let's take a look at each side and then see what the Bible shows us in Jesus.

Truth

On one side, we have people who hold to truth alone. These people often have strong convictions and high standards. They clearly see right and wrong. This helps when making tough decisions. However, there is a tendency to also make life tough in general. They want people to change, but they don't always allow for mistakes and growth. The focus on this end is being right.

Grace

On the other side, we have people who hold to grace alone. These people are nice to be around. They help us feel better about ourselves. They accept us for who we are. However, there is also the tendency not to encourage us to be what we could (and should). They might demand nothing, but they also get nothing. The focus on this end is being loved.

Jesus

What does the Bible have to say about truth and grace? In John 1:14, it tells us Jesus Christ came *"full of grace and truth."* Jesus was fully grace and fully truth. And we see this to be true in His life. In truth, He spoke out against hypocritical religious leaders. He talked about the coming judgment and mentioned both heaven and hell. He set a high standard for His disciples. In grace, He welcomed sinners, outsiders, the hungry, the hurting and the "unclean." He had compassion. He was forgiving and full of love. Jesus was both truth and grace because, really, the two go hand in hand. Jesus said, *"you will know the truth, and the truth will set you free"* (John 8:32). Only when we are faced with truth (that we are sinners) can we receive sweet grace and be set free.

What does this mean for us?

In the words of Pastor Kevin Deyoung, "We need to be grace people and truth people. Not half grace and half truth. Not all grace on Mondays and all truth on Tuesdays. All grace and all truth all the time." [1]

Week Two

Colossians 1:15-17

CHRIST IS BEFORE ALL THINGS.

Many scholars agree that Colossians 1:15-20 has a poetic structure to it. Some even suggest it was an early hymn. It is wonderful to see how sometimes Truth is best represented in artistic form. Today we are going to find truth at the highest source.

To begin, Colossians 1:15 says that Christ is the "_____ *of the invisible God."*

This word *"image"* has the same meaning as when I say my niece is the spitting image of her father. Their looks, mannerisms and personalities are all alike. In this way, Christ is the spitting image of God.

What did Jesus say in John 14:9?

Colossians 1:15 goes on to say that Christ is also *"the _____ of all creation."*

This is not to say that Christ was "born" or "created." Rather, this original term signified birthright or the primary heir of the family.

We further know the term above does not mean Christ was "created" because verse 16 says that *"by him _____ things were _____."* What specific things does verse 16 go on to mention?

From verse 16, we can rightly say that Christ created the highest angels in heaven, as well as the tiniest atoms on Earth. He created all the things we can see, as well as all the things we cannot see (like gravity, for instance.) The thrones, dominions, rulers and authorities might refer to the order of angels, meaning cosmic powers in the spiritual realm. Or it might refer to earthly international powers, politics and economics. Either way, all of creation came from Christ. It was created *"through him and for him"* (v. 16). *"Through him"* might better be translated "to him," meaning to give Him glory. *"For him"* refers to His future, forever, ultimate reign over creation. Absolutely everything ... everything ... is from and for Christ.

What does Philippians 2:9-11 tell us will one day be the response of all creation?

In the space below, copy the words of Colossians 1:17, replacing the pronouns with Who they represent (Jesus).

Jesus is *"before all things"* (v. 17). This means He both came first and reigns first. Jesus also holds all things together. Multiple scholars have worded it as something like, "Jesus prevents creation from falling into chaos."

> A divided world can often feel like chaos. Have there been moments lately where you feared the world was falling apart? What does it mean to you to know the truth — that Jesus is in control, right now, in these very moments?

Praying Colossians 1:15–17

TAKE A MOMENT TO ACKNOWLEDGE CHRIST'S AUTHORITY. LAY DOWN YOUR CONCERNS AND TROUBLES AT HIS FEET TODAY AND DECLARE THE TRUTH: CHRIST *"IS BEFORE ALL THINGS, AND IN HIM ALL THINGS HOLD TOGETHER"* (V. 17). PRAY FOR GOD TO HELP YOU REMEMBER THAT.

Colossians 1:18–20

CHRIST IS PREEMINENT.

Yesterday we mentioned how Colossians 1:15-20 appears to be poetic in structure and may even be one of the first Christian hymns. Let's finish our look into these verses today by talking about Christ's preeminence. *Bible Sense Lexicon* defines the word *"preeminent"* (v. 18) as "ranking above all others" or "to be first."[1] Today's reading shows Christ is preeminent in three major ways.

CHRIST IS PREEMINENT IN THE CHURCH

Colossians 1:18a says that Christ is the "_____ of the _____, the *church.*" Take a moment to draw this out in the space below. Draw a circle to represent God, as the head of the Church. Now draw arms, legs and a torso representing us, the Church. It can be a stick figure or something more intricate. Drawing uses the right side of your brain and will help you remember these truths. What is the function of a head for the body?

This is vital for the Church to remember. Christ comes first. We have **no other leader.** All other leaders are subordinate leaders. No pastor, elder, pope or priest is the leader of the Church. Nor is any monarch, president, government or political party. And while we should absolutely be respectful of these positions (see Hebrews 13:17 and 1 Peter 2:13-15), we also remember that the Church has only one Head. What does this mean to you in regard to knowing the Truth in a world of divided opinions?

CHRIST IS PREEMINENT IN RESURRECTION

Colossians 1:18b goes on to say that Christ is *"the beginning, the firstborn from the _____..."*

We know there are stories in the Bible of others who were raised from the dead. However, Jesus' resurrection was different. Jesus was the first to raise to life in a glorious, incorruptible body that could never again die. [2] And this is the type of resurrection we, too, will one day receive. How does 1 Corinthians 15:35-42 describe the future resurrected body?

CHRIST IS PREEMINENT IN RESURRECTION

Colossians 1:19-20 is especially poignant in this letter because these verses touch on some of the false teachings that were threatening the early church. One such false teaching was the idea that Christ was one of many "spiritual journeys" a person could take. After all, Christ was just a man, right?

Yet what does verse 19 say?

Christ was not just another man. He was fully man, but He was also **fully** God. Another false teaching floating around was the idea that all earthly things were evil, and only spiritual things could be redeemed.

Yet verse 20 says that, through Christ, He reconciled to Himself "_____ *things, whether on* _____ *or in heaven...*"

colossians

This means Christ's redemption is for everything. Yes, Jesus saves in the spiritual realm. But Jesus is also working and redeeming in the nitty-gritty, messy, everyday parts of today. There is no limit nor anything beyond His ability to save.

What in your life needs Christ's redemptive work today?

Praying Colossians 1:18–20

LET'S PRAY FOR THE CHURCH TODAY, OUR BROTHERS AND SISTERS AROUND THE GLOBE. PRAY WE WOULD BE UNITED UNDER ONE HEAD. PRAY SPECIFICALLY FOR SOMEONE TODAY WHO NEEDS TO BE REMINDED THAT JESUS' RESURRECTION HAS FREED THEM FROM THE FEAR OF DEATH. PRAY FOR CHRIST'S REDEMPTIVE WORK TO MOVE AND STIR THROUGH YOUR LIFE SITUATION. MAY HIS WILL BE DONE.

HYMNS OF THE NEW TESTAMENT

Words are one of the most fundamental ways we communicate. Because we were made in the image of our creative God, there is something that happens when we use our words to create something beautiful or meaningful. When creating poetry or music, words have a way of communicating that is layered and deep.

It is no wonder that we see music and poetry throughout the Bible. The Old Testament is full of songs and hymns, some of praise, some of lament. In fact, the entire book of Psalms is devoted to these ancient works. One of these hymns Jesus Himself sang with His disciples at the Last Supper. (Matthew 26:30) Can you imagine hearing the voice of Jesus singing in praise to His Father?!

The first-century Church also sang. In fact, it is in Colossians that we see Paul encouraging Christians to sing *"psalms, hymns and spiritual songs"* (Colossians 3:16). History tells us the early Church took these words to heart. Around the year A.D. 111, a Roman governor named Pliny the Younger was investigating the "error" of Christians and reporting back to the emperor Trajan. In his letter, he wrote: "They had met regularly before dawn on a fixed day to chant verses alternately among themselves in honour of Christ as if to a god." [1] In the earliest days of the Church, music and hymns had become a part of worship. Biblical scholars have identified sections of Scripture they believe to be examples of early Christian hymns. One of these we see in Colossians 1:15-20. It is possible that this "hymn" was written by Paul, but most agree that it was more likely adapted by Paul from a hymn previously written by another apostle, prophet or early church leader. Just think of early Christian song writers putting Truth into rhyme, rhythm and notes so that it could be remembered, shared and used for praise!

On the pages that follow, you will see a list of passages that many scholars believe are early Christian hymns in the New Testament.[2] As you read these passages, imagine our first brothers and sisters gathering together, reciting and singing these words of Truth. Although now translated into English, you can still feel the rhythm and cadence of the words. What a beautiful look at Truth in artistry.

WHAT IS ONE OF YOUR FAVORITE WORSHIP SONGS THAT HELPS REMIND YOU OF TRUTH?

COLOSSIANS 1:15-20

He is the image of the invisible God, the firstborn of all creation.
For by him all things were created, in heaven and on earth, visible and invisible,
whether thrones or dominions or rulers or authorities—
all things were created through him and for him.
And he is before all things, and in him all things hold together.
And he is the head of the body, the church.
He is the beginning, the firstborn from the dead, that in everything he might be preeminent.
For in him all the fullness of God was pleased to dwell,
and through him to reconcile to himself all things,
whether on earth or in heaven, making peace by the blood of his cross.

JOHN 1:1-5

In the beginning was the Word,
and the Word was with God,
and the Word was God.
He was in the beginning with God.
All things were made through him,
and without him was not any thing made that was made.
In him was life,
and the life was the light of men.
The light shines in the darkness,
and the darkness has not overcome it.

PHILIPPIANS 2:6-11

who, though he was in the form of God, did not count
equality with God a thing to be grasped,
but emptied himself,
by taking the form of a servant,
being born in the likeness of men.
And being found in human form,
he humbled himself by becoming obedient to the point of death,
even death on a cross.
Therefore God has highly exalted him
and bestowed on him the name that is above every name,
so that at the name of Jesus
every knee should bow,
in heaven and on earth and under the earth,
and every tongue confess that Jesus Christ is Lord,
to the glory of God the Father.

EPHESIANS 2:14-16

For he himself is our peace,
who has made us both one
and has broken down in his flesh the dividing wall of hostility
by abolishing the law of commandments expressed in ordinances,
that he might create in himself one new man in place of the two,
so making peace,
and might reconcile us both to God in one body
through the cross,
thereby killing the hostility.

1 TIMOTHY 3:16

Great indeed, we confess, is the mystery of godliness:
He was manifested in the flesh,
vindicated by the Spirit,
seen by angels,
proclaimed among the nations,
believed on in the world,
taken up in glory.

2 TIMOTHY 2:11-13

The saying is trustworthy, for:
If we have died with him, we will also live with him;
if we endure, we will also reign with him;
if we deny him, he also will deny us;
if we are faithless, he remains faithful—
for he cannot deny himself.

HEBREWS 1:3

He is the radiance of the glory of God
and the exact imprint of his nature,
and he upholds the universe by the word of his power.
After making purification for sins,
he sat down at the right hand of the Majesty on high,

1 PETER 3:18

For Christ also suffered once for sins,
the righteous for the unrighteous,
that he might bring us to God,
being put to death in the flesh
but made alive in the spirit,

Colossians 1:21-23

ONCE HOSTILE, WE ARE NOW RECONCILED.

Today let's look at three areas of life when it comes to the truth: where we were, where we can be and how to stay on the right path.

WHERE WE WERE

Colossians 1:21 uses an interesting word to describe where we once were.

It says we *"once were _____..."*

The word *"alienated"* can also mean "estranged" or "having lost closeness." Our sin has alienated us from God. We were separated; we lost closeness with the Source of all Truth.

Also according to verse 21, we were *"_____ in mind, doing _____ deeds."*

To be *"hostile"* is to be the enemy, to be openly opposed. This is our condition before Jesus. *Life Application New Testament Commentary* says, "When people are out of harmony with God, their natural condition is to be totally hostile to his standards." [1]

In what ways can we see that the world around us seems to be alienated from, or out of harmony with, God?

WHERE WE CAN BE

Before Jesus, we were hopeless in our mess and sin. We were alienated from God. We were hostile enemies jumping toward evil. However, Colossians 1:22 reminds us of the Good News we now have in Christ. Jesus has reconciled us. He has restored our closeness.

According to verse 22, Jesus has reconciled us **how**? *("by his _____ ")*

Jesus has reconciled us **why**? *("in order to...")*

Because of Jesus, we can once again be in the presence of God. This can only happen if we are blameless, holy and above reproach. And while we can be none of these on our own, Jesus gives us this position freely and lovingly.

HOW TO STAY ON THE PATH OF TRUTH

We have established that we were once alienated from God and hostile. Then, in Christ, He has freely given us His blameless, holy covering so we can be close to God once again. But God's Word in Colossians clarifies that this free gift does not mean we can live carelessly. Rather, we should *"continue in the faith"* (v. 23).

What words does verse 23 use to describe how our faith should (and should not) look?

This particular section is once again touching on the issue of false teaching. The Colossian Christians were being tossed around from one teacher to the next, each teacher having a different opinion about what was actually true regarding Christ and the Church. Paul wanted to make clear that their faith was tethered to one Truth, the gospel of Christ. And if we want to make sure that our faith is stable, steadfast and not shifting, we, too, must hold everything up to the truth of God's Word and character. When neighbors, politicians, coworkers, pastors or anyone comes up to us with information or insight, we have to filter everything we see, hear or think through the truth of the gospel. This is how we will stand firm. This is how we will know the truth and not be tossed around by divided opinions.

> Write in your own words how you will both know and stand stable and steadfast in the truth, in the faith, in the hope of the gospel.

Praying Colossians 1:21–23

PRAY FOR THOSE YOU KNOW WHO ARE ALIENATED AND HOSTILE IN MIND TO THE FATHER. PRAY THAT THE RECONCILIATION OF CHRIST WOULD COME TO THEM. LET'S ALSO PRAY FOR OURSELVES AND OUR FAMILIES, THAT WE WOULD CONTINUE IN THE FAITH, THAT OUR FAITH WOULD BE STABLE AND STEADFAST, NOT SHIFTING FROM THE HOPE OF THE GOSPEL.

Colossians 1:24–29

WE REJOICE IN SUFFERING AND MATURE IN CHRIST.

Today's reading starts with verse 24, which can be confusing at first glance. Let's break it down to get a better understanding.

Colossians 1:24 says, *"Now, I _____ in my _____..."*
Do you view suffering this way? Why or why not?

Verse 24 goes on to say that in suffering, we are *"filling up what is"* what?

This does not mean that Christ's suffering work on the cross was insufficient or "lacking" in any way. There is nothing we can add to the salvation that Christ achieved for us. So what exactly is Paul saying here?

Let's look at the end of verse 24. Paul says he is taking on sufferings for the sake of what?

As the Church, we are the **body** of Christ. We are one with Him. And what Christ has endured, so do we. We share in His sufferings. Our *"flesh"* (as Paul says in verse 24) continues on with Christ's suffering until He comes again and all suffering will be complete. In this sense, the only thing that is "lacking" is the continued suffering of the Church as it awaits Christ again. And Paul says he has taken on plenty of this pain. You and I do as well.

I appreciate N.T. Wright's comment on this. He says, "... all Christians will suffer for their faith in one way or another: if not outwardly, then inwardly, through the long, slow battle with temptation or sickness, the agonizing anxieties of Christian responsibilities for a family or a church, ... the constant doubts and uncertainties which accompany the obedience of faith, and 'the thousand natural shocks that flesh is heir to', taken up as they are within the call to follow Christ." [1]

> In what ways are you sharing in Christ's sufferings as well? And how does *"Christ in you, the hope of glory"* (v. 27) help you rejoice?

In this study, we are on a quest to know the truth. Sometimes finding truth feels like having to solve a mystery, where the answer is just out of our grasp. Today's reading talks about a "mystery" as well. It was the mystery of God's plan. The people of the Old Testament were given clues (a Messiah would come, and God's Kingdom would be established forever), but they didn't understand.

> However, there is no longer any "mystery" to solve. Verse 26 says *"the mystery hidden for ages and generations"* is now what? Also, in verse 25, Paul says he was appointed to help *"make the word of God"* what?

According to verse 27, God chose to make known to everyone this mystery. What is the answer to the mystery?

What does this teach you in your quest to know the Truth? Will it be hidden from you?

Write in big, bold letters the first phrase of verse 28, stopping at the comma.

For Paul, the end goal was not simply to get people to make a profession of faith in Christ (though that is certainly important!). Paul warned and taught *"with all wisdom"* (v. 28). And it is by this wisdom that Paul wanted the church to learn and grow in the Truth because he wanted to *"present everyone _____ in Christ."* What do you think this word means?

In what ways are you helping to *"mature"* the Church?

Praying Colossians 1:24–29

LET US PRAY FOR THOSE WHO ARE SUFFERING TODAY. PRAY FOR THEM BY NAME, THAT CHRIST WOULD BE IN THEM, FILLING THEM WITH THE HOPE OF GLORY, GIVING THEM A REASON TO REJOICE TODAY. LET'S PRAY ALSO FOR THE MATURING OF THE CHURCH, THAT THERE WOULD BE NO "MYSTERY" TO THE GOSPEL BUT THAT TRUTH WOULD BE REVEALED AND FULLY KNOWN.

Colossians 2:1–5

IN CHRIST, WE FIND WISDOM AND KNOWLEDGE.

In today's reading, we see the word *"struggle"* (Colossians 2:1). The Greek word used here (*agōn*) gives the idea of an athletic contest. It means to go out and fight. [1] Every day, we wake up, and we take up the "struggle." We work, stress, train and fight. We do this for ourselves, our families, our friends, our neighbors — maybe even occasionally for people we have never met (like Paul is doing here for the Colossians and Laodiceans).

Who do you *"struggle"* for and in what ways (v. 1)? What do you hope to achieve from that?

Paul says he struggled greatly for those at Colossae and Laodicea so that they might what, according to verse 2?

I find Matthew Henry's insight interesting: "[Paul] does not say that they may be healthy, and merry, and rich, and great, and prosperous; but that their *hearts may be comforted*. The prosperity of the soul is the best prosperity, and what we should be most solicitous about for ourselves and others." [2]

In what ways might you focus your daily *"struggles"* even more toward soul prosperity?

Colossians 2:2 talks about the riches of what two things?

To emphasize what we talked about yesterday, what, again, is *"God's mystery"* (which is a mystery no more)? (Colossians 2:2)

And in Christ we find what two specific treasures? (v. 3)

The text alludes to the problem of false teaching that affected the Colossian church. (v. 4) These untruths infiltrated the church, causing division and problems. This is why today's reading emphasizes that understanding and knowledge are **riches**, and wisdom and knowledge are **treasures**. Knowing the Truth would safeguard the church from these false teachers. In his commentary on Colossians, Charles Swindoll says, "Because Jesus alone is the treasure trove of wisdom and knowledge (2:3), the only way false teachers can persuade people to buy their fool's-gold philosophies is to turn attention away from Christ and toward their fabulous fabrications." [3]

> From what we have learned today, what is one major way that we can detect false teaching or untruth?

Sometimes when we cannot be in the same location as someone else, we tell them, "I am with you in spirit." This is the exact phrase Paul uses in Colossians 2:5; however, this was not just some cliché for him. For all of us as Christians, we are truly knit together by the Holy Spirit. This means we have spiritual unity and togetherness, even when we are physically separated.

> Does this change your view of the phrase "with you in spirit"? Even though we might be physically separated, we are still united by the Spirit. Who can you encourage today with this good news?

Praying Colossians 2:1–5

WHO CAN YOU PRAY FOR TODAY, THAT THEIR *"HEARTS MAY BE ENCOURAGED"*? WHAT DIVISIONS CAN YOU PRAY FOR THAT MIGHT BE *"KNIT TOGETHER IN LOVE"* (V. 2)? PRAY THAT ALL OF OUR WISDOM AND KNOWLEDGE WOULD BE FOUND IN CHRIST AND THAT WE WOULD RECOGNIZE FALSE TEACHING WHEN WE HEAR IT. PRAY FOR ANYONE YOU MISS TODAY BECAUSE OF PHYSICAL DISTANCE BUT ARE TOGETHER WITH IN SPIRIT.

Weekend Reflections

For our weekends in this study, we'll take some of the dividing opinions we hear, and look at them through the truth of God's Word.

This week, we talked about Christ and His greatness. All the mystery of God's plan, all wisdom and knowledge can be found in Christ. And through His sacrifice, He reconciled us. He brought us back close to Him. We didn't do the work; it was Christ alone. Yet this free gift does not mean we get to live careless lives. How do we balance the grace of forgiveness and the discomfort sin brings to our conscience?

For Week 2, read the section titled **"Condemnation vs. Conviction"** on page 58.

Have you witnessed division in terms of condemnation and conviction? Where specifically?

What do you learn about the truth from God's Word?

How can you walk in the Truth this week?

Condemnation vs. Conviction

There can sometimes be divided opinions concerning the words "condemnation" and "conviction." Both of these words are biblical, but they can be misunderstood and misused. Let's look at what the Bible has to say.

Condemnation

Many of us have heard Romans 8:1, which says, *"There is therefore now no condemnation for those who are in Christ Jesus."* However, look carefully at the qualifier to this statement. There is no condemnation **only for those who are in Christ** — meaning there is such a thing as condemnation. We clearly see this when Jude 1:4 tells us that condemnation stands ready for the ungodly who deny Jesus. In John 3:18, Jesus himself says whoever does not believe in the Son of God *"is condemned already."* What we learn from this is that biblical condemnation is more than a feeling. It is a state of being that defines your relationship with God. [1] To be "condemned" means that your eternal home is not with God. It means you have been found guilty of sin and sentenced to death. This sounds scary, and it is! But pretending it isn't real doesn't help us.

This is where the rest of Romans 8:1 is so powerful. Without Jesus, we have condemnation, but IN Christ Jesus, there is none. Our state of being is IN relationship with God. Our eternity is secure in Him.

Conviction

Now, just because as Christ-followers we no longer have any condemnation, this does not mean we will not feel guilty over sin. One of the roles of the Holy Spirit is to convict us of sin. (John 16:8) Our sin will weigh on us, as the psalm says, like a *"heavy burden"* (Psalm 38:4). This conviction is for a purpose. In Psalm 38:18, conviction led David to say, *"I confess my iniquity; I am sorry for my sin."* Biblical conviction acknowledges sin and leads to repentance. It is a gift from God that helps guide and protect us.

What does this mean for us?

Second Corinthians 7:10 says, *"For godly grief produces a repentance that leads to salvation without regret..."* Biblical conviction focuses on our wrong behaviors and leads us to repentance. In conviction, we can say, "I made a wrong choice." This then turns us back toward our loving Father for correction and help. Let's not shy away from this precious gift from the Lord.

Biblical condemnation, on the other hand, is about identity. If our identity is outside of Christ, we remain condemned for our crimes against God's law. However, there is no condemnation for those who are in Christ, the One who fulfilled the requirements of God's law. Therefore, as Christ-followers, we must guard against condemnation. And we can recognize condemnation because it attacks our identity. It makes us say things like "I'm a terrible person." It leads us away from our loving Father, making us want to hide in shame.

In Summary

Condemnation: Real. But not for Christ-followers.
Conviction: Good for us all.

Week
Three

Colossians 2:6-7

WE ARE ROOTED IN CHRIST.

Today's reading is filled with metaphors and imagery, so we are going to do something a little different. We are going to go through the verses and create a drawing, and then afterwards we will dissect what we learn from this.

To begin your drawing on the following page, start with a tiny seed in the middle of the page, planted in soil. Colossians 2:6 talks about that moment when we *"received Christ Jesus the Lord."* Label your seed as "Received Christ." Verse 6 says we then *"walk in him."* Just as a new baby must learn to take steps, we, too, must learn how to walk in Christ. Draw a sprout from your seed that pierces the soil. Label it "Learning to walk." Now verse 7 says we need to be *"rooted."* Draw numerous roots sprouting out from the seed underground, going multiple directions. Label this "Rooted." Not only are we rooted, but we are also *"built up"* (v. 7). Turn your sprout above the soil line into a plant of some type. Label it "Built up." This metaphor from Paul is actually that of a building being built off of its stable foundation. Even this metaphor reminds us of the importance of the ground. Verse 7 goes on to say we are *"established in the faith."* Under the ground near your roots, write "Faith." Verse 7 says *"just as you were taught,"* and Colossians 1:23 told us we were taught *"the hope of the gospel."* Near your roots, write "Hope" and "Gospel." Finally, verse 7 finishes with *"abounding in thanksgiving."* The natural result of these will be gratitude. Near the top of your plant, write "Thanksgiving." Now's let's make some observations.

The word *"received"* is in the past tense (v. 6). There was a past moment when we received Christ. However, *"walk"* is in present tense (v. 6). It is something we do today, continuously. In other words, the past event of receiving Christ becomes a present reality in our lives every single day. In what ways does your relationship with Jesus affect your everyday life?

Let's talk for a moment about roots. What is the purpose of roots in a plant? (Being a farmer's wife, I'll give you some clues. Where does a plant get water and nutrients? Also, what keeps a plant upright, especially in the wind?) How does this apply to your Christian walk?

Looking at these verses (and your drawing), what grows strong roots for a Christian?

colossians

Without strong roots, a tree/flower/crop would blow over on the next windy day. Tomorrow we'll talk about these "winds," but to help us prepare, what "winds" can you think of that might threaten to uproot people of faith today?

I love how verse 7 ends by talking about *"abounding in thanksgiving."* When we are rooted in the faith and hope of the gospel of Jesus, when we truly understand all that He has done for us, we cannot help but overflow with gratitude. Take a moment to think about the truth of the gospel message. What thoughts of thanksgiving begin to bubble up within?

Praying Colossians 2:6–7

TODAY, LET'S PRAY FOR THE YOUNGER GENERATIONS. PRAY THAT THESE GENERATIONS WOULD BE **ROOTED** AND BUILT UP IN CHRIST, ESTABLISHED IN FAITH AND TAUGHT THE TRUE GOSPEL. PRAY FOR SOMEONE BY NAME TODAY. FINALLY, EXPRESS TO GOD THE FATHER YOUR ABOUNDING THANKSGIVING FOR THE GIFT OF HIS SON.

rooted

Colossians 2:8–10

EMPTY, DECEITFUL PHILOSOPHIES CAN LEAD US ASTRAY.

The goal of our Colossians study is to discover how to know the Truth in a world of divided opinions. Today we'll see two divides that affected the church in Colossae and how both were wrong.

Colossians 2:8 starts, *"See to it that no one takes you..."* what? (This word was often used in Greek to refer to the plundering of cargo ships. It meant to snatch up, to steal away.)

According to this verse, what can we be taken captive by?

When we see these terms in verse 8, we can think *"philosophy"* and *"empty deceit"* are two separate things. However, the language used in Greek binds them closer together than that. In its most basic definition, "philosophy" means "love of wisdom." And there is nothing wrong with wisdom and education! What this verse is saying is that we need to watch out for *"empty"* and *"deceit[ful]"* philosophy — any thought or ideology that leads away from the truth is dangerous. This verse shows two divisive ideas that were full of this kind of philosophy.

Read the remainder of verse 8. What three *"according to"* phrases are listed (in ESV)?

On one end of the spectrum, Colossians often heard those teaching according to *"human tradition"* (v. 8). It seems this phrase in particular was a reference to Jewish laws and customs. The Jewish community was putting pressure on the church to conform to their rules and regulations. However, the Law of the Old Testament was there to show us we are incapable of living perfectly. It is tempting to try to earn our salvation, as if it could be ours to attain by our might and our greatness. But this could never be the case. We cannot enter heaven and God's presence by "being a good person."

In what way is following rules and traditions in order to feel good about ourselves and to secure our salvation actually an empty and deceitful philosophy?

On the other end of the spectrum, Colossians faced teachings of the *"elemental spirits of the world"* (v. 8). This is an interesting phrasing, and most scholars agree that it likely refers to pagan religions and their "gods" or perhaps even demonic spirits. Paganism appealed to the flesh. It pushed sex, money and power. It made promises. "If you keep your end of our little bargain…" it said. It made you feel like you had some control over the world.

In what ways is following the *"elemental spirits of the world"* and our flesh an empty, deceitful philosophy?

The only teaching that is not empty and deceitful is Christ's.

According to verse 9, what dwells in Him bodily?

The end of verse 10 says He is the Head of what?

Christ is fully God. All of the truth about God that the Jewish people found in the Old Testament was in Christ. Christ is also the Head of all rulers and authorities. All other "gods" and powers bow to Him. And Colossians 2:10 says that WE *"have been filled in him."* When we are in Christ, we have His strength, His power and His Truth. And nothing can steal us away or lead us astray in Him.

> This is a difficult question, but take a moment to think about the world around you. Can you identify any empty, deceitful philosophies that are threatening to take you captive? What might Jesus speak in authority and Truth over those philosophies?

Praying Colossians 2:8–10

PRAY THAT WE WOULD NOT BE TAKEN CAPTIVE BY PHILOSOPHY AND EMPTY DECEIT! PRAY THAT THE CHURCH WOULD STAND SECURELY ON THE TRUTH THAT IS CHRIST. PRAY THAT WE WOULD BE FILLED IN HIM. WHO CAN YOU PRAY FOR BY NAME TODAY — THAT HE OR SHE WOULD BE FILLED WITH CHRIST?

Applying God's Word Today:

HOW TO SPOT (AND STOP) FALSE TEACHING

One of the problems facing the church in Colossae was the influence of false teachers. There were people teaching additions to the gospel that were not in line with Christ, and Paul made it his mission in this letter to warn against such false information.

Just as it was for the church in Colossae, false information can also be an issue for the Church today. So how do we spot (and stop) false teaching as Christians?

When we come across information, the first thing we should do is assess its believability. Is it consistent with what we know to be true? In the Church, we have the added gift of the Holy Spirit to guide us in Truth. (John 16:13) If we hear a teaching that does not sit right with us, do we dig in to understand why? Are we paying attention to the promptings of the Spirit — those gentle stirrings and nudges that prick our conscience? These warning signals are gifts from the Spirit.

The second step to spotting false teachings is to examine the source. In society, we have what are referred to as primary and secondary sources. Primary sources are the immediate, firsthand accounts. This is pure information. Secondary sources, on the other hand, are one step removed from the information. These sources will (hopefully) access primary sources but will often put their own analysis on the information. Obviously, the farther away you go from the primary source, the more layers and opinions get added to that information. And like in the "telephone game," it can sometimes come out on the other side as a totally different message than when it started. So when taking in information, pay attention to the sourcing. In the Church, our primary source is the Bible. It is so important that we read it and know it well. Our secondary sources will be our pastors, teachers and, yes, even this Bible study in your hands. Hopefully, we are all doing our best to stay true to the primary source, but it is up to YOU to check. Check those Bible references. Check that teaching against the Scriptures. Is the information you receive always, always, always lining up with the Word of God?

Now we know how to spot it, so how do we stop false teachings from spreading?

Number one: Let's not take information at face value. We need to stop, to think, to pray, to research. Pay attention to the nudging of the Spirit, ask good questions and check everything against our primary source, the Bible.

Number Two: Let's not repeat/share/repost/reteach any information until we have done so. Let's be known for sharing only the Truth.

WHAT ARE SOME OF YOUR FAVORITE "SECONDARY SOURCES" FOR SPIRITUAL INFORMATION? DO YOU STOP TO CHECK THEM AGAINST THE PRIMARY SOURCE (THE BIBLE)? WHY OR WHY NOT?

Colossians 2:11–15

WE WERE DEAD IN SIN BUT ARE MADE ALIVE IN CHRIST.

Today's reading starts with a metaphor that would have specifically made sense to Jews: **circumcision.**

Colossians 2:11 says, *"In him also you were circumcised with a circumcision made* _____ _____, *by putting off the body of the* _____, *by the circumcision of* _____." Let's look at these three elements.

Under the Old Testament, circumcision was the removal of flesh that marked a special covenant with God. It was a physical sign that you were one of God's chosen people. Read Galatians 6:15. Under the new covenant of Christ, what is the worth of physical circumcision?

In Christ, we have a new kind of "circumcision." It is marked by cutting away the sinful nature. It is now a spiritual procedure — where the mark of the commitment is written on our hearts, not on our bodies. And because it is now a spiritual procedure, there is only One who can perform this procedure. We must have Christ do this job for us. How does knowing this help us better understand that salvation is truly from Christ alone?

Now today's text is going to use the symbolism of **baptism**. Baptism is the act of being immersed in water.

Going down underneath the water in baptism is a symbol of *"having been ..."* what, according to Colossians 2:12? (This shows there has been a death of our old self.)

Coming back up out of the water in baptism is a symbol of being *"_____ with him through faith..."* (v. 12). (This shows we are resurrected to a new life.)

From there, the text brings these two images together into a new image. See, if you were a gentile, you had two problems going for you. First, you were physically uncircumcised (and thus not in special relationship with God). Second, you were *"dead in your trespasses"* (v. 13). But God did an extraordinary work. He put an end to all the divisions and separations!

Colossians 2:13 says, ***"God made _____ _____ with him..."***

God took down the divisions caused by sin: the ones between us and Him, and the ones between "us" and "them." Now we are all together ... with Him. What joy. And all because He has *"forgiven us all our trespasses"* (v. 13). Verse 14 talks about *"the record of debt."* This term specifically refers to a handwritten note labeling someone's offense.

Imagine seeing every sin, every unkind word, every unpleasant thought you've had, handwritten by God Himself on a note in front of you. What thoughts come to your mind?

When Romans executed criminals by crucifixion, they would often nail the "record of debt" to that person's cross, showing those passing by what crime that person had committed.

Read the account in John 19:19-22. What record of debt was posted on Jesus' cross?

According to Colossians 2:14, what other record was nailed to Jesus' cross?

If anyone deserved to be put to "open shame," it would be us with our long lists of offenses. However, those lists were nailed to the cross, and Jesus took on that shame instead. And in doing so, He *"disarmed the rulers and authorities and put **them** to open shame, by triumphing over them in him"* (Colossians 2:15, emphasis added).

Which of the images from today's study stood out to you, and why?

Praying Colossians 2:11–15

PRAY THAT CHRIST WOULD CIRCUMCISE OUR HEARTS. PRAY THAT OUR OLD SELVES WOULD BE BURIED WITH CHRIST AND THAT WE WOULD LIVE EVERY DAY AS A PEOPLE WHO HAVE BEEN RAISED TO LIFE. THANK HIM FOR NAILING OUR TRESPASSES TO HIS CROSS AND FOR TRIUMPHING OVER THE ENEMY.

Colossians 2:16–19

LET NO ONE JUDGE OR DISQUALIFY YOU, BUT HOLD FAST TO CHRIST.

Today's verses take us into the gritty details of the opinions and false teachings that threatened to divide the church in Colossae. We have a lot of ground to cover today, so let's jump right in!

Yesterday we learned that in Christ we have victory. Colossians 2:16 starts with the word *"Therefore..."* In other words, the sentence that comes next in verse 16 is **because** of the victory and forgiveness and salvation in Jesus Christ we just learned about.

With these things in mind, *"Therefore..."* let no one do what (v. 16)?

This phrase *"pass judgement"* is more than just to judge and condemn. It specifically means to "exclude." There were systems and teachings taking place that were telling people they were excluded from God if they didn't look or act a certain way.

Why is it wrong to tell anyone they are excluded from God's plan and love? (See John 3:16.)

In this passage, there are two teachings specifically that were attempting to pass judgement or exclude.

1. Food and Drink: This is a reference to Jewish kosher laws of the Old Testament. There were many items a Jew could not eat or drink. Pharisees through the years had taken these laws and added to them. A rule about not cooking a goat in its mother's milk turned into a rule about never consuming milk and meat together at the same time. [1]

2. Jewish Holy Days: This list in verse 16 encompasses everything from yearly festivals to monthly new moons and weekly Sabbaths. These holy days separated Jews from their gentile neighbors. "But wait," you might say. "Does this mean we shouldn't keep a 'Sabbath?'" Let's get to the heart of the problem here ... legalism.

Legalism is an excessive adherence to and dependence on moral law. Under the Old Covenant, the Law was all the people had. However, verse 17 calls this a *"shadow of things to come."* Imagine you see a shadow in the shape of the Empire State Building. This was the Law. There was no color, detail or tangible way to touch, climb or dwell inside of it.

According to verse 17, Who is *"the substance,"* or the real thing, that the shadow merely represented?

One dividing opinion circulating among the Colossians was that they needed to follow the Old Testament ceremonial laws or else they would be excluded from God. But the truth is, **the Law doesn't save us. Only Jesus saves.** How might legalism be affecting the Church today?

Now let's look at the second set of false teachings hurting the church at Colossae.

The second section of this text (starting in verse 18) says, *"Let no one..."* do what?

This phrase *"disqualify"* meant to tell people that they "weren't qualified." They were not enough. Not spiritual enough, not smart enough, not having the "spiritual insight" that others had.

Why is it wrong to disqualify anyone from God's love and plan? (See 1 Corinthians 1:27.)

In this passage, there are two teachings specifically that attempted to disqualify people.

1. Asceticism: This word means a practice of strict and severe self-denial for personal and religious purposes. Scholars agree that, in this particular verse, it appears to refer to a type of extreme fasting that was supposed to induce heavenly visions (as is mentioned later in this verse).

2. Worship of Angels: This could have a couple of different meanings. We know from artifacts discovered from this time period that some people wore amulets around their necks with inscriptions asking the angels for protection. [2] So it could mean a tendency to call on angels for help or safety. Another suggestion is that Paul could be using a form of irony. Some people were spending so much time and energy thinking about, studying and speculating on angels that it was practically like worshiping them! What is the root of these teachings? Mysticism.

Mysticism is the belief that union with God or spiritual knowledge inaccessible to the intellect may be attained through an inner religious experience, as opposed to through God and His Word. In this belief, only a special few had a mystic experience and were then "enlightened."

But according to Colossians 2:18, these kinds of teachings only make a person "_____ _____ *without* _____ *by his sensuous mind...*"

The problem with such a teaching is it exalts lesser things. By proclaiming special knowledge or status with God (because of some ritual or self-denial), a person is actually puffing up themselves. When we lift up ourselves, our brains and our experiences, or when we lift up angels or amulets, anything that we lift up other than Jesus will draw us away from *"the Head"* (v. 19) ... away from the only One who is worthy of being lifted high! How might mysticism be sneaking into the Church today as well?

Let's end with a couple of conclusions.

Legalism threatens to exclude us from both God and each other. But verse 19 says Christ is our Head and we, the Church, are the body, and we are being *"nourished and _____ together ..."*

Mysticism threatens to tell us that we need special experiences and knowledge to grow spiritually. But verse 19 says that in Christ we grow *"with a growth that is _____ _____."*

Praying Colossians 2:16–19

PRAY THAT THE CHURCH WOULD BE PROTECTED FROM LEGALISM AND PASSING JUDGMENT. PRAY THAT THE CHURCH WOULD BE PROTECTED FROM MYSTICISM AND TELLING OTHERS THEY ARE DISQUALIFIED. PRAY, INSTEAD, THAT WE WOULD BE KNIT TOGETHER, BE NOURISHED THROUGH CHRIST, GROW WITH A GROWTH THAT IS FROM GOD, AND ONLY LIFT HIGH AND HOLD FAST THE NAME OF JESUS.

SET YOUR MINDS ON THINGS THAT ARE ABOVE,
NOT ON THINGS THAT ARE ON EARTH.

COLOSSIANS 3:2

Colossians 2:20–23

BEWARE OF HUMAN TEACHINGS THAT
APPEAR RELIGIOUS BUT HAVE NO VALUE.

Yesterday we talked about some of the false teachings affecting the church in Colossae. Today we'll see why these teachings are sneaky and why they have no value.

Colossians 2:20 starts off by saying, *"If with Christ you died to the..."* what?

In Colossians 2:8 we talked about the *"elemental spirits of the world"* being pagan gods, evil spirits and the ways of the world. In Christ, we died to these things. We are no longer under their power. We are no longer slaves to them. So, Paul asks, why would we submit to them again? (v. 20) First let's look at what was luring believers away.

What three rules or "regulations" are mentioned in verse 21?

Very important to note, these rules were given *"according to ..."* what? (v. 22)

As Christians, we only serve one master. We only listen to one voice. First and foremost, above all else, above <u>anyone</u> else, we follow the voice of Truth, Jesus Christ.

What are some helpful voices speaking into your life?

What are some harmful voices speaking into your life?

Whose voice is speaking the loudest?

colossians

All of these rules were sneaky. Matthew 7:15 says, *"Beware of false prophets, who come to you in sheep's clothing but inwardly are ravenous wolves."*

These harmful rules were sneaky because they appeared to be what, according to Colossians 2:23?

What a reminder to always be on our guard when it comes to Truth! What does 1 Thessalonians 5:21 teach us?

Colossians 2:23 says these rules and practices *"are of no value ..."* Let's talk for a moment about what gives rules value.

I am a rule-follower. I actually *like* rules. I like knowing what is expected. But I am reminded today it's not all about the rule but rather the heart behind the rule. Am I following rules to appear wise — to look good and holy and right? Or am I following rules to obey and love God? Do I make choices or go into action because someone along the way told me "this is what we do" or "don't do"? Or because God's Word and Spirit direct me, and I respect, trust and love God's boundaries He sets for me? Am I imposing rules on others that God has not ordained for them? Rules themselves can be good and helpful, but they only have value if they come from God and are obeyed from a heart overflowing with love for Him.

Take an assessment of your attitude toward rules. Are you a natural rule-follower or rule-resistor? What might be the unique challenges for each? What have you learned or what stood out to you from today's reading?

Weekend Reflections

As we have mentioned, we'll spend our weekends looking at some of the dividing opinions we hear and how we can know the Truth through God's Word.

This week, we talked about the false teachings that were attempting to lead the church astray. Some of these teachings were "worldly" in nature; some were "spiritual."

For Week 3, read the section titled **"Worldly Wisdom vs. Spiritual Wisdom"** on page 86.

Have you witnessed division in terms of worldly and spiritual wisdom? Where specifically?

What do you learn about the truth from God's Word?

How can you walk in the Truth this week?

Worldly Wisdom vs. Spiritual Wisdom

As we have been talking about divided opinions throughout this study, perhaps the area of "worldly wisdom" vs. "spiritual wisdom" feels pretty obvious to you. This is a Bible study, after all, so the spiritual side must be better, right? However, I hope our study through Colossians causes us to stop and take the time to think about what is the Truth. Let's explore both sides.

Worldly Wisdom

Before we begin on worldly wisdom, let's define the difference between knowledge and wisdom. Knowledge is simply knowing facts. Wisdom, on the other hand, is applying those facts in the best way for life. So when we talk about worldly wisdom, we are not referring to simply the facts. Science has taught us much about cells, the solar system, human DNA and energy flow, just to name a few things. Facts are fascinating (because we have a fascinating Creator)! When the Bible talks about worldly wisdom, it is referring to how we live our lives, specifically for ourselves. And when we live to lift up ourselves, the Bible says it is *"foolish," "folly"* and *"futile."* (1 Corinthians 1:20; 3:19) This worldly wisdom is the very opposite of true wisdom.

Spiritual Wisdom

King Solomon was told he could have anything he asked of God. He asked for wisdom, and it pleased God to grant him this and more. Yet notice what Solomon writes at the end of his life in Ecclesiastes 1:17. He says, *"I applied my heart to know wisdom and to know madness and folly. I perceived that this also is but a striving after wind."* Wait, what? Solomon said applying wisdom was as useless as chasing the wind?! Remember, wisdom is how we apply to our lives what we know. We can observe Solomon's life and see that, as time went on, he started to elevate himself, his power, his wealth and his desire for more wives. Could it be that the wisest man to ever live actually lacked true wisdom? (See 1 Kings 11:4.) In Colossians we have learned that we must be on the guard against things that have *"an appearance of wisdom"* (Colossians 2:23). Even so-called "spiritual wisdom" must be held to the Word of God for accuracy.

What does this mean for us?

Our King, Jesus, gave us two commands: to love God and to love others. (Matthew 22:35-40) So real wisdom is to apply everything we know to accomplishing these two tasks. Bible teacher Jen Wilkin doesn't pull any punches when she says, "Simply put, any thought, word or deed that compromises our ability to love God and neighbor is folly. Utter foolishness. The height of stupidity." [1] Anything at all that presents itself to us as wisdom, worldly or spiritual, must pass through this test to be true. Does it help me love God and others? If the answer is "yes," then I'm on my way to becoming a little wiser.

Week Four

Colossians 3:1-4

OUR LIFE IS CHRIST.

As we move into the last two chapters of Colossians, today's reading serves as a bridge between the issues of false teachers to now living in a manner that is pleasing to the Lord. Even with the bridge, we learn an important lesson. Once you know the Truth, as we say here at Proverbs 31, "it changes everything." Really knowing, grasping and understanding the Truth will affect how you live.

In what ways does how we live reflect what we know and believe?

Colossians 3:1 starts out by saying, *"If then you have been raised with Christ..."* This instantly brings out two major points.

Very specifically, this letter is intended for whom?

This also reminds us that, once, we were dead, but now we are what?

The Greek word for *"seek"* in verse 1 means to try to find something with the intention of possessing it. It is seeking to own. The Greek word for the phrase *"Set your minds"* in verse 2 means more than to simply ponder. It means to **believe** and to **honor**. [1]

Colossians 3:1 says we are to seek what? Verse 2 says we are to set our minds on what?

What (or rather, Who) is above? (According to verse 1, He is seated at the right hand of God.)

Verse 3 spells out again that we have died, and our life is now *"hidden"* with Christ. This word "hidden" means protected or kept safe. When you look at the world around you, what does it mean to you to know you are "hidden" in Christ?

Can we talk for a minute about today's culture? Research has shown that the millennial and Gen Z generations are characterized by high and rising anxiety. More than any other generation! Science has been trying to discover why. Some say it is decision making. There are more options than ever before, and the weight of having to analyze those many options is heavy. Some say it is the need to be better and get farther than the previous generations, which appear to be failing. There seems to be a theme of needing to do more, be more, achieve more. To be better than yesterday and better than "them." If this is you, can we maybe help lift a burden off your shoulders today with the truth of Scripture? This may sound oversimplified, but if you let it, it can be freeing. You have only one goal in life. Only one.

Colossians 3:4 says, *"When _____ who _____ _____ _____ ..."*
Take a moment to look at the words you have written down.

The one goal, in the life of a people who have died to the world and been raised to life in Christ, is to follow Christ. Christ is our life. To look like Him, act like Him and love like Him. And this may look like fewer trophies or ribbons, less money or fame, on Earth. But I think we can look around and see that all of those things are failing us anyway. They are *"things that are on earth"* (Colossians 3:2). Our gaze is different. Our goal is different. And our prize at the end is way better.

As Christians, *"When Christ who is your life appears, then you also will..."* what? (v. 4)

Praying Colossians 3:1–4

PRAY THAT WE WOULD *"SEEK"* THINGS ABOVE (V. 1). PRAY THAT WE WOULD *"SET [OUR] MINDS"* (V. 2) AND BELIEVE IN AND HONOR THINGS THAT ARE ABOVE. PRAY THAT OUR ONE GOAL IN LIFE WOULD BE CHRIST. LORD, HELP US TO DIE TO EARTHLY THINGS. LET US BE HIDDEN WITH CHRIST. THANK HIM FOR THE PROMISE OF ETERNITY WITH HIM IN GLORY.

colossians

Colossians 3:5–11

WE PUT TO DEATH WHAT IS EARTHLY IN US.

Yesterday we said that life is Christ. Today we'll look at things that are not life. In fact, if we see any of these things in ourselves, we should put them to death. The lists from today's reading can be broken down into two categories: sexual sins and anger sins.

Because our study on Colossians is looking into the world of divided opinions, I want to share this quote from N.T. Wright on this particular passage. He says, "Many Christians tend to concentrate on one list or the other: one knows of Christian communities that would be appalled at the slightest sexual irregularity but which are nests of malicious intrigue, backbiting, gossip and bad temper, and conversely, of others where people are so concerned to live in untroubled harmony with each other that they tolerate flagrant immorality. The gospel, however, leaves no room for behavior of either sort." [1]

> In thinking of this quote, why can we not pick and choose which truths we want to apply? And why might Jesus' words in Matthew 7:3-5 be important as we study today's text?

Let's look at the first group of earthly things we need to hunt out in our lives and put to death: sexual sins. (Use Colossians 3:5 to fill in the blanks.)

> *"Put to death therefore what is earthly in you:* _____ _____..." This is any form of sex outside of marriage.

> "..._____..." This is moral uncleanness. Perhaps no sexual act has taken place, but the person has a crudeness or insensitivity to sexual purity.

"..._____..." According to *Strong's Greek Dictionary,* the Greek word used here (*pathos*) specifically refers to sexual passions or "lust." These are uncontrolled sexual urges. [2]

"..._____ _____..." The term can sometimes mean "cravings." It is a continual want for something not good for you. Let's take a moment to talk about the difference between evil desires and temptation. Temptation, even sexual temptation, is not a sin. (See Hebrews 4:15.) However, sin begins when a temptation that has presented itself in our minds is not at once put to death. In the words of N.T. Wright, it is instead "fondled and cherished." [3]

"... *and* _____..." This is greed or an unchecked hunger for physical pleasure.

The big problem with these, as with most sins, is *"idolatry."* What, or who, might be the idol in sexual sin? Why might this be a problem?

Sin hurts us, and it hurts those around us. And a good and holy God cannot allow it. While verse 6 might seem harsh, deep down I think we all are truly glad that this is Truth. Sin (either ours or others') and its harmful consequences will not torment us forever because...

Write the words from Colossians 3:6.

Now let's look at the second group of earthly things we should put to death: anger sins. (Use Colossians 3:8-9 to fill in the blanks.)

"But now you must put them all away: _____..." This is a smoldering hatred that lives under the surface.

"..._____..." Sometimes the word used is "rage." It is when anger explodes in either words or deeds.

"..._____..." This is an evil that deliberately intends to hurt another person.

"..._____..." Often an outlet for malice. It is hurting someone or their reputation with words.

"... and _____ _____ *from your mouth."* This is speech that is dirty, crude, abrasive or filled with expletives.

And verse 9 says, "_____ _____ _____ *to one another..."* This means "untruth." Sometimes the truth can be uncomfortable or inconvenient. But because we know the Truth, as Christ-followers, we constantly speak the Truth.

Which of these sticks out to you as you examine your own heart?

We put off the old, dead ways. And we put on our new self. This isn't easy. And there will be times when we mess up. I think that is why I love the wording of verse 10. It says our new self *"is being renewed…"* This is present tense. Today. We get a fresh start. We can try again. And we do this by being renewed *"in knowledge"* (in Truth, in Jesus) *"after the image of its creator."* We know Jesus, so we can look and act more like Jesus. A little more every day. It's true for you. And for me. And for our brothers and sisters around the globe. All of us, together, working to be like Jesus.

In big, bold letters, write the last six words of Colossians 3:11 (ESV).

Note: For a deeper look into Colossians 3:11, see the additional content **"The Great Divides."**

Praying Colossians 3:5–11

PRAY TODAY FOR YOUR OWN HEART AND FOR THE HEARTS OF THOSE YOU LOVE — THAT THEY WOULD BE FREE FROM SEXUAL IMMORALITY AND IMPURITY. THAT TEMPTATIONS WOULD TURN NOT INTO EVIL DESIRES BUT WOULD BE IMMEDIATELY SQUASHED AND DEALT WITH. PRAY THAT ANGER WOULD DISSOLVE AND HURTS WOULD BE HEALED. PRAY THAT MOUTHS WOULD BE HOLY AND PURE, AND THAT LIES WOULD NOT STAND. PRAY FOR RENEWAL AND UNITY, AS *"CHRIST IS ALL, AND IN ALL"* WHO PUT THEIR TRUST IN HIM (V. 11).

Applying God's Word Today:

THE GREAT DIVIDES

Colossians 3:11 gives us an excellent overview of some of the major divides that have plagued the earth throughout time. Look at the chart below to see the verse and the divides it mentions. Take a moment to think how and where these apply to our world today.

COLOSSIANS 3:11	THE GREAT DIVIDE	HOW IT LOOKS TODAY:
Greek and Jew	Racial/National Divides	
Circumcised and Uncircumcised	Religious Divides	
Barbarian or Scythian (These were names used for people unfamiliar with Greek language and culture. They were called "uncivilized.")	Cultural Divides	
Slave or Free	Economic/Social Divides	

Colossians 3:11 says that in Christ, these don't exist. That is not to say that once we become a Christian, we are no longer of our ethnicity, church affiliation, upbringing or economic class. Rather, these things **do not divide us** in Christ. We all come as we are, and in Jesus' sight we are equal in worth. Why? Because Christ is in us all. And **He is all.** Let's reach out to someone on the other side today, a fellow brother or sister in Christ, and together let's bridge the great divides.

Colossians 3:12-15

WE PUT ON VIRTUES OF CHRIST.

Yesterday we talked about the sins that needed to be put to death in our lives. Today we are going to look at the flip side and see what virtues need to be put on. This term *"put on"* used in Colossians 3:12 was often used to describe getting dressed or "putting on" a garment. These virtues should be the clothes we wear every day. Remember when we said our goal in life is to be like Christ? Here is what that looks like.

Right off the bat, today's reading says **we** are God's chosen ones, holy and beloved. Who is the Chosen One in 1 Peter 2:4? Who is the Holy One in John 6:69? Who is the beloved in Matthew 3:17?

Using Colossians 3:12 as our guide, let's fill in the virtues we wear.

The first virtue we are to put on is that of "_____ _____." This means a deep sensitivity to the needs and sorrows of others. In Exodus 22:25-27, we are told that God is compassionate. Read this passage and write down what compassion means to you.

The second virtue we put on is "_____." This means acting benevolently towards others. It means we look up from our own little worlds to see, think of and act graciously toward other people. Ephesians 2:4-7 teaches us that God is kind. Read this passage and write down what you observe about kindness.

The next virtue we put on is "_____." This is not thinking too highly or too lowly of oneself. It is knowing our position with God: sinners, saved and forgiven by grace alone. Philippians 2:5-11 shows us the humility of Jesus. Read this passage. What does this remind you about humility?

The next virtue we put on is "_____." This is a gentleness that requires great strength. It is a willingness to give up one's rights for the sake of other people. Jesus Himself talks about His meekness in Matthew 11:29. What does meekness look like?

The final virtue of verse 12 is "_____." Particularly in this passage, it means a patience toward others. This is an ability to put up with people who irritate. This fruit is from the Spirit, so His work in us will increase our endurance. Second Peter 3:9 says the Lord is patient. Read this passage. What do you learn about patience?

Colossians 3:13 urges us to work on *"bearing with one another ..."* This means making allowances for people's faults. It means restraining your reactions. The verse goes on to talk about *"forgiving each other; as the Lord has forgiven you..."* (v. 13). We forgive because we remember how much we have been forgiven and because we understand that God forgives.

Take a moment to ask God if there is any area in your life where you might need some work on *"bearing with one another"* or *"forgiving each other"* (v. 13). What is one step you can take today?

Colossians 3:14 says, *"And above all these put on..."* Let's stop there for a moment. This is garment language again. This next word is going to be like the belt. It is going to go over the top and cinch everything together and hold it in place.

According to verse 14, what do we put on above all these?

Love is what binds all of these virtues together. We cannot pursue the others without love, or they will become distorted and unbalanced.

Why might love need to be applied to all the virtues listed above?

Colossians 3:15 says, *"And let the peace of Christ rule in your hearts..."* The peace referred to here is not "inner peace" or "peace of mind." It is a direct reference to peace among people (as is evidenced when the verse says we were called to *"one body"*). The word *"rule"* used in this verse is an athletic term. It was like an umpire or a referee. The peace of Christ was to arbitrate and decide arguments. *Life Application New Testament Commentary* says, "To live in peace would not mean that suddenly all differences of opinion would be eliminated, but it would require that they work together despite their differences." [1]

What stands out to you about peace? How does this verse apply to our study's title, *How To Know the Truth in a World of Divided Opinions?*

All of these help us to look more like Jesus. It is not easy, but it is good. And we have the Holy Spirit to help us.

To end today, write the last two words of Colossians 3:15. This is the mindset we need every morning when we get up and "put on" Christ.

Colossians 3:16–17

WE DO EVERYTHING IN THE NAME OF JESUS.

In this study, we have been talking about how to know Truth. We established early on that all wisdom and knowledge is found in Christ. We find Truth when we look to Christ and His Word. Now that we know where to find the Truth, today's verses are going to show us what to do.

Colossians 3:16 says, *"Let the word of Christ dwell in you richly..."* This word "dwell" means to "live permanently." Even more, it means to "be at home in." [1]

How might you know if God's Word is at home in you? What does that look like?

The Word of God speaks truth into our lives in many ways. Two such ways are teaching and admonishing (which simply means to warn or caution).

What specific ways do you take in God's Word, receiving its teaching and admonishing? (For example: personal Bible reading, church podcast, etc.)

Traditional teaching and study is not the only way in which God's Word speaks Truth.

What other mediums are listed in verse 16, after *"teaching and admonishing one another in all wisdom..."*?

What specific songs can you name that have taught and reminded you of truths from God's Word?

It is difficult for us to fathom God's Word without the New Testament. At the time of this letter, the Church did not have the gift of the New Testament. They had some letters that were passed around, people who came and told them about this man named Jesus, and others who would share words that Jesus had said. Because they did not have a written New Testament to reference, many times these words and truths about Jesus were put into song to help believers remember and memorize them. It is a method for memorizing we still use today. (Am I the only one who remembers the order of the books of the Bible by using a song?) Music is powerful in many ways. I also love the distinction between the three words New Testament scholar Douglas Moo notes: "It is attractive to identify 'psalms' as songs based on Scripture, 'hymns' as songs about Christ, and 'songs' as spontaneous compositions 'prompted by the Spirit.'" [2]

Do you think of Truth as being manifested through music or other forms of art? Why or why not?

Verse 16 ends by saying *"with thankfulness in your hearts to God."* Truth, whether learned through teaching, admonishing, psalms, hymns or other spiritual songs, always leads to praise. Truth points us to Christ, who is worthy of all our worship.

Fill in the blanks

Let's take a quick look back at yesterday. Colossians 3:15: *"And let the peace of Christ rule in your hearts, to which indeed you were called in one body. And _____ _____."*

And now for today's reading. Colossians 3:16: *"Let the word of Christ dwell in you richly, teaching and admonishing one another in all wisdom, singing psalms and hymns and spiritual songs, _____ _____ in your hearts to God."*

Colossians 3:17: *"And whatever you do, in word or deed, do everything in the name of the Lord Jesus, _____ _____ to God the Father through him."*

The truth is found in God's Word. It is Christ. And we allow Him to dwell in us richly. When we do, it changes our lives. Chapter 3 of Colossians has spent a lot of time telling us specific things not to do, as well as specific things to do. But the goal of Colossians is not to make a list of "do's" and "don'ts." If we are not careful, we could become legalistic, which Paul specifically warned the church against. Instead, verse 17 sums up for us our entire "rule book" as Christ-followers.

Read verse 17 again, slowly. How does this verse sum up our lives, our choices, our words, deeds, opinions and actions?

Praying Colossians 3:16–17

TODAY LET'S PRAY FOR BIBLE TEACHERS AND PASTORS. FOR BIBLICAL SPEAKERS AND WRITERS. FOR BIBLICAL MISSIONARIES AND EVANGELISTS. FOR BIBLICAL MUSICIANS AND ARTISTS. PRAY THAT THEY WOULD BE USED BY GOD TO HELP THE WORD OF CHRIST DWELL RICHLY AMONG US. PRAY THAT EVERY WORD YOU SPEAK, EVERY THOUGHT YOU THINK, EVERY MOVEMENT AND ACTION AND BREATH, WOULD BE DONE IN THE NAME OF THE LORD JESUS. GIVE THANKS TO HIM. GIVE THANKS TO HIM AGAIN.

Old Self vs. New Self

OLD SELF	NEW SELF
SEXUAL IMMORALITY	CHOSEN
IMPURITY	HOLY
PASSION	BELOVED
EVIL DESIRE	COMPASSIONATE HEARTS
COVETOUSNESS	KINDNESS
IDOLATRY	HUMILITY
ANGER	MEEKNESS
WRATH	PATIENCE
MALICE	BEARING WITH ONE ANOTHER
SLANDER	FORGIVING
OBSCENE TALK	LOVE
LIES	HARMONY
	PEACE
	THANKFULNESS
	WISDOM
	SINGING

Colossians 3:18–4:1

LET'S LOOK LIKE CHRIST IN OUR HOMES.

Today's passage has been abused and misused. It has been hated and disregarded. If we want to talk about divided opinions, there are plenty surrounding these verses. However, I don't want us to walk into these verses with any opinions. Let's approach them only as a means of seeking Truth. Let's decide up front that we will set our cultural biases aside and let only the Bible, not society, have the authority to speak into how we live.

Home. It's the place where we are probably our most true self. So if we want to work on truly being more like Christ, we start with our positions in the home.

> Take a moment to think about your home. How would you describe it? What are your roles in the family? Are you married, a parent or a child? How would you describe those relationships?

Colossians 3:18-19 is going to start with marriage. Verse 19 would have been quite unpopular for Roman society. During the time this was written, husbands had harsh, **absolute power.** Today, verse 18 is quite unpopular in modern society. Much has been done in the last century to help empower women, for which I am so grateful. Christ Himself treated women in an honoring and empowering way. However, sometimes "empower" can twist itself into a quest for **"absolute power."** And in either case, **absolute power** is dangerous. C.S. Lewis once said, "If the home is to be a means of grace it must be a place of rules ... the alternative to rule is not freedom but the unconstitutional (and often unconscious) tyranny of the most selfish member." [1] To avoid tyranny and selfishness of either husband or wife, let's take a look at these rules presented in Colossians.

Verse 18 says wives are to *"submit to [their] husbands..."* The word "submit" does not mean becoming a doormat. It means there is not a constant battle for power in the relationship. It also means considering others before yourself. What are some practical, everyday ways that wives can show godly submission?

Verse 18 adds, *"as is fitting in the Lord."* How might submission actually help us look more like Jesus?

Before we go on, it is important to point out a fundamental aspect of submission. Read Ephesians 5:21. This verse is directed to all Christ-followers. What does this verse teach us about submission?

Verse 19 says husbands are to *"love [their] wives, and do not be harsh with them."* We mentioned earlier how in Roman culture, harsh power was considered a husband's cultural "right." While the surrounding culture might have thought that was OK, hurting others is never OK with God. Therefore, here in Colossians, we see a call to lay down what society calls "our rights" for the good of others. What examples can you think of where someone gave up their societal "rights" for the good of someone else?

Ephesians 5:28 explains more on what it looks like for husbands to love their wives. Read this verse. If we want to look like Christ, what does love look like?

One last note before we move on. Read Jesus' words in John 13:34. This verse is also directed to all Christ-followers. What does this verse teach us about love?

Colossians 3:20-21 looks at the parent/child relationship. The word for children (*tekna*) was a reference to young children living at home. I love N.T. Wright's comment that "in addressing children as members of the church, ... and in giving them both responsibilities and rights, Paul is again allowing the gospel to break new ground." [2] Children are important to Christ!

What does Jesus say in Matthew 19:14?

Children are to *"obey [their] parents in everything..."* (v. 20). This means there is to be discipline within the home. Children are to be taught. Read Hebrews 5:8. How is obedience being like Christ?

Once again, we have a balance presented. Yes, children need discipline, but so do parents. The word *"fathers"* in verse 21 is a term that referred to both parents. The word *"provoke"* refers to constant nagging or belittling. A parent's job is to assure children that they are loved and "valued for who they are, not for who they ought to be, should have been, or might (if only they would try a little harder) become." [3] And obedience should never be a condition for a parent's love. Jot down some ideas of things that might "provoke" and "discourage" a child. Now write an equal number of ways to love and encourage a child. Circle one of these supportive ideas and find a child to encourage.

Colossians 3:22-4:1 looks at the relationship between bondservants and masters. In ancient Rome, enslaved people and household servants played a significant role in society. It is true that this passage neither condemns nor condones slavery. However, the fact that this passage addressed enslaved people directly, as fully human, with dignity, did send a message.

Lest we think this passage no longer applies to us, take a moment to read Philippians 2:5-7, Romans 6:22 and Mark 10:45. What do you learn about servanthood, Jesus and yourself?

How should we serve, according to Colossians 3:22?

To what tasks, big or small, important or mundane, can you apply verse 23 today?

When we serve others, who are we ultimately serving, according to verse 24?

Once again, we are given a balance. Masters were to *"treat [their] bondservants justly and fairly ..."* (Colossians 4:1). In other words, see and treat them as human beings. Part of that was realizing that the masters, too, had a Master in heaven, and remembering how He had treated them. While none of us are "masters" today, the principles still apply. In what ways can we stop today and truly **see** the person on the other side of the counter, window, phone or computer as a human being ... and then treat them as such?

Praying Colossians 3:18–4:1

TODAY, LET'S PRAY FOR THE WIVES WE KNOW, THAT THEY WOULD RESPECTFULLY AND WILLINGLY SUBMIT, EVEN WHEN IT'S HARD. LET'S PRAY FOR THE HUSBANDS WE KNOW, THAT THEY WOULD SACRIFICIALLY LOVE AND BE GENTLE, EVEN WHEN IT'S HARD. PRAY FOR CHILDREN YOU KNOW, THAT THEY WOULD LEARN TO RESPECT AUTHORITY IN THEIR LIVES. PRAY FOR PARENTS (AND TEACHERS!) YOU KNOW, THAT THEY WOULD NOT PROVOKE OR DISCOURAGE BUT WOULD LOVE, VALUE AND SHOW CHILDREN JESUS. PRAY FOR THE SPIRIT OF A SERVANT TO RISE UP IN THE HEARTS OF EVERY BELIEVER, STARTING WITH YOURSELF. FINALLY, PRAY THAT THE SPIRIT WOULD QUICKEN YOUR HEART TODAY TO STOP AND REALLY SEE THE PERSON IN FRONT OF YOU.

colossians

Weekend Reflections

Let's continue our look at divided opinions and how we can know the Truth through God's Word.

This week, we learned how we can look more like Jesus. Some of these concepts go against the grain of our culture and society.

For Week 4, read the section titled **"Humility, Meekness, Submission and Servanthood vs. Modern Society"** that starts on page 114. Choose one of the four words to study, and answer the questions below.

Have you witnessed division in terms of the concept you studied? Where specifically?

What do you learn about the truth from God's Word?

How can you walk in the Truth this week?

Humility, Meekness, Submission and Servanthood vs. Modern Society

When we think about divided opinions, there are few words that are looked down on more than the four words "humility," "meekness," "submission" and "servanthood." Modern society does not always value these as positive traits. And while the Bible clearly teaches these concepts, even among Christians there can be confusion about what exactly these words entail. Let's take each word and break it down to understand the truth.

Humility

Pastor Paul Carter gives us an excellent, biblical look into humility by breaking down what humility both is and is not. [1]

Biblical humility **is not:**
- Insecurity (not knowing who you are). (1 Corinthians 15:10)
- Indecisiveness (not making solid decisions, being wishy-washy). (Matthew 11:7-11)
- Inactivity (hiding your talents, doing nothing). (Matthew 25:26-30)

Biblical humility **is:**
- A complete dependence on God's mercy (knowing your sinfulness and need for a Savior). (Luke 18:10-14)
- An unconcern for power, prestige or position (definitely not a common worldview). (Matthew 23:8-12)
- An unquestioning acceptance of God's Word (just like Jesus *"humbled himself by becoming obedient,"* even though it meant death on a cross [Philippians 2:6-8]).

Meekness

To use a common dictionary, the word "meekness" brings up words like "quiet," "overly submissive," "shy" and "timid." [2][3]

However, to understand biblical meekness, we need to take a look at it in its Greek form and place it within the context of Scripture. When we do this, we find that "meekness" actually means "a total lack of self-pride," as well as "a decided strength of disciplined calmness." [4]

Meekness is making a decision to stay calm when your emotions want to react. It is strength under control. It refers to "those who do not assert themselves over others in order to further their own agendas in their own strength ... they trust in God to direct the outcome." [5]

Submission

For this word, I particularly appreciate John Piper's breakdown of what submission "is not." [6] Here, we are going to look at six wrong assumptions about submission to help us eliminate any incorrect ideas that we have picked up. For this particular breakdown, Piper uses 1 Peter 3:1-6 as a reference and speaks directly toward women in marriage (which is the context in which we saw this word used in Colossians 3:18). However, Ephesians 5:21 tells all Christ-followers to submit to everyone, so this list actually applies to us all.

- **Wrong Assumption:** Submission means agreeing on everything.
  (There are some situations where it is OK to disagree. For example, the wife in 1 Peter 3:1-6 disagreed with her husband on not following Jesus.)
- **Wrong Assumption:** Submission is leaving your brain at the altar.
  (Submission means being a team player, and all team members should bring their thoughts, ideas and talents to the table.)
- **Wrong Assumption:** Submission means you do not try to influence and that you simply accept the decisions that are made.
  (Submission is a calling to honor and affirm leadership, yes, but it also means to help carry that leadership according to your own spiritual gifts as well.)
- **Wrong Assumption:** Submission is putting the will of others before the will of Christ.
  (We always, always follow Christ first.)
- **Wrong Assumption:** Submission means your spiritual strength should come from the other person.
  (Living in submission does not make our spiritual growth and strength dependent on anyone else. For example, while traditionally the husband is the spiritual leader in the home, this is not always the case. A wife can guide her family in growing in Christ as well, whether or not there is someone in the home helping in this regard.)
- **Wrong Assumption:** Submission is living or acting in fear.
  (Nowhere in the Bible does it suggest that we submit to abuse. If you, or someone you love, are in a relationship that is characterized by hurt, shame or fear, please seek the help you need to be safe. You are God's beloved child.)

So what is a good definition of biblical submission? Let's look to Jesus, who submitted to the Father's will. He left heaven to come down to us. He gave His life for us. Submission is an act and attitude that puts others before ourselves.

Servanthood

Often the world tells us to make a name for ourselves or to set our eyes toward climbing the ladder to the top. Yet the Bible is clear about the importance of servanthood in Christ-followers. With a little help from unlockingthebible.org, let's look at biblical servanthood. [7]

- To be a servant is to be humble (like how Jesus washed feet). (John 13:12-16)
- To be a servant is to prepare. (We should practice and train to serve.) (1 Timothy 4:7)
- To be a servant is to persevere. (Serving can be a long, tiring, thankless work, but we continue knowing that Jesus is coming soon!) (Luke 12:35)
- To be a servant is to serve where needed. (That might mean abroad or across town, and it also might change with the day — i.e. one day you change a tire, the next a diaper. A servant simply lives to serve whoever, wherever, whenever.) (1 Corinthians 9:19-23)
- To be a servant is to serve (or not serve) as God directs. (King David wanted to build God a temple, but God told him "no." We serve only where God leads.) (2 Samuel 7:1-17)
- To be a servant is to expect to suffer. (It will be painful at times. It will cost us. But we always have Jesus as our example.) (Matthew 10:24-25)
- To be a servant is to be unashamed. (Servants of God can lift their heads high, even in the midst of lowly work.) (2 Timothy 2:15)

Week Five

Colossians 4:2–4

CONTINUE STEADFASTLY IN PRAYER.

Friends, we have made it to the final week of our study, the last chapter of Colossians and the wrap-up to this letter. Today's focus is prayer.

Let's break down Colossians 4:2 into three parts.

"Continue steadfastly ..." This phrase in Greek also means to "persevere devotedly." It is both continuous and consistent. Charles Swindoll gives an excellent description of this phrase. He says, "Prayer is to be active, not passive; bold, not weak; specific, not general; attentive, not lazy; continuous, not sporadic." [1]

> Which of these words might describe your prayers? What is one step you can take this week to help your prayers *"continue steadfastly"*?

Swindoll goes on to say, "We acknowledge that He [God] has the power to give us what we ask but the right to answer however he pleases. And we can know that however He answers – 'Yes,' 'No,' 'Wait,' or 'Here's something better' – He's going to work everything out for our good, not for our harm." [2]

> How does Romans 8:28 give us reassurance as we continue on in prayer?

*"**Being watchful in it ...**"* The Greek word for *"watchful"* means "to be alert, be awake, and to keep watch." In regard to prayer, we watch for situations and people to pray for, watch for God's answers to our prayers, and *"[stay] awake,"* ready for His return (Matthew 24:43).

These words in Colossians are an echo of Jesus' words to His disciples. Read Mark 14:38. What word does Jesus pair with prayer?

What does "being watchful" look like to you?

*"**With thanksgiving.**"* You may notice an attitude of thanksgiving has been a theme of Colossians. It is especially important to include thanksgiving in our prayers. As the *ESV Study Bible* points out, "Thanksgiving leavens prayer, so that it does not become merely a selfish pleading to have one's desires fulfilled." [3]

In what ways might thanksgiving discourage selfishness?

Paul specifically asks for prayers for himself in the next section of today's reading.

When was the last time you asked someone to pray for you specifically?

What does he ask for? (vv. 3-4)

Interesting. Paul simply wanted opportunities to clearly share the gospel ... while still in prison. He knew there were no chains on the Good News. Also amazing is that we have good reason to believe that the Colossians' prayers for Paul in this capacity were answered!

Read Acts 28:30-31. What do we learn about Paul's time in prison?

One final note for today. Paul had a very specific request. He wanted to share the *"mystery of Christ"* (which is simply that Christ is for everyone, gentiles included), but he wanted to *"make it clear"* (Colossians 4:3-4). The last thing he wanted to do was complicate the gospel or make it confusing. Perhaps, with his academic mind, this was something he personally worried about. We don't know specifics. But we do learn from this exchange that it is good to pray for missionaries, leaders, pastors and others in ministry. Even more, let's pray for them by name and in ways that are specific to their circumstances.

Who might you be led to pray for specifically today?

Praying Colossians 4:2-4
LET'S PRAY FOR HELP IN OUR PRAYER LIFE. HELP TO BE STEADFAST AND WATCHFUL AND THANKFUL. PRAY FOR SOMEONE BY NAME WHO IS OUT SHARING THE GOSPEL. PRAY FOR DOORS TO OPEN FOR THEM TO SHARE THE WORD. PRAY THAT THEY WOULD SPEAK IT CLEARLY. END YOUR PRAYER TODAY BY THANKING GOD FOR THREE SPECIFIC THINGS IN YOUR LIFE.

Colossians 4:5-6

WALK IN WISDOM AND TALK WITH SEASONING.

Yesterday we looked at prayer and our talk with God. Today we are going to look at our walk and talk with *"outsiders"* (Colossians 4:5). Specifically, this means people who are not Christians, also called "unbelievers."

> In what situations in your life do you have interactions with unbelievers? Do you have a relationship with anyone who is not a Christian? Why or why not?

The first part of today's reading addresses how we **walk.** The Greek word translated as "walk" means to act, live or behave. It involves the actions of daily life.

> According to Colossians 4:5, we are to walk (act, live, behave) in what?

True wisdom, as we have learned, is only found in God. Therefore, to *"walk in wisdom"* (v. 5) is to live according to God's standards. And while this is simply the best way for us to live our lives for ourselves personally, living this way is also crucial when it comes to "outsiders." I love this quote from Charles Swindoll: "We're wrong to expect unbelievers to live like Christians, but they are right to expect Christians to live like Christ." [1]

Why might it be so important for Christians to *"walk in wisdom toward outsiders"* (v. 5)?

Verse 5 ends with *"making the best use of the time."* In other words, every day that God gifts us on Earth is an opportunity to be a witness to the outside world. We do not know how much time we, or others, have left.

How does this tie in with Psalm 90:12?

The second part of today's reading addresses our **talk**. Verse 6 says to *"let your speech always be gracious..."* "Gracious" means kind, but it also is a reference to God's grace. Our speech should demonstrate God's goodness, love and forgiveness. Our speech is also to be *"seasoned with salt"* (v. 6). The use of salt was a common metaphor during this time. In this particular usage of the word, it means "flavorful." What does "flavorful" speech look like? Scholars agree it means:

- Interesting. And not boring.
- Interactive, where others are listened to and allowed discussion.
- Colorful, adding zest, flavor or depth to the conversation.

Scottish minister William Barclay said it this way: "It is all too true that Christianity in the minds of many is connected with a kind of sanctimonious dullness and an outlook in which laughter is almost a heresy ... Christians must commend their message with the charm and wit which were in Jesus himself. There is too much of the Christianity which stodgily depresses people and too little of the Christianity which sparkles with life." [2]

Who do you know who speaks this way well? What is it that makes their speech flavorful or *"seasoned with salt"* (v. 6)?

In what ways might you improve the conversations you have? What can you remove and what can you add?

Finally, Colossians 4:6 ends with *"so that you may know how you ought to answer each person."* In other words, our speech is knowledgeable. We cannot share the Truth if we do not know the Truth personally. It is so important for us to know the Truth found in God's Word. It is also important to remember that if we are **walking** like Jesus and **talking** like (and about) Jesus, people outside are going to ask questions.

> If someone were to ask you today why you seem different than other people, how might you answer? Is your answer gracious and seasoned with salt?

Praying Colossians 4:5–6

PRAY TODAY FOR THOSE IN YOUR CLOSEST IMMEDIATE CIRCLE, BY NAME. PRAY THAT THEY WOULD WALK IN WISDOM. PRAY THEIR WALK WOULD BE A WITNESS TO OUTSIDERS. PRAY THAT THEIR SPEECH WOULD BE GRACIOUS AND SEASONED WITH SALT. PRAY THAT THE HOLY SPIRIT WOULD HELP GUIDE THEM TO ANSWER EACH PERSON IN LOVE, TRUTH AND GRACE.

Colossians 4:7–9

BOTH VETERAN MINISTERS AND NEW CONVERTS CAN SPREAD THE GOSPEL.

Today we begin what is known as the final greetings. Paul often ended his letters with greetings to and from particular people he mentioned by name. It is so important that we remember these letters were sent to real-life people, just like you and me. Let's get to know the first two people Paul mentioned.

Tychicus
We learn from Colossians 4:7 that, more than likely, this letter was going to be sent to the church in Colossae through a man named Tychicus. What an important task, to hand-deliver a Spirit-inspired letter from the Apostle Paul! And this wasn't the first time.

Read Ephesians 6:21-22. Where else did Tychicus go?

Read 2 Timothy 4:12. What do we learn here?

Read Titus 3:12. Who else was Tychicus possibly headed to see? (This person was located somewhere near Crete.)

Read Acts 20:4. What citizen of Asia Minor accompanied Paul on his journey to Jerusalem?

Tychicus was a trusted companion to Paul. He delivered many important letters, helping spread the gospel across the known world. Now let's look at his character.

> Colossians 4:7b says Tychicus was a:
> "..._____ _____..." (fellow Christian).
> "and _____ _____..." (someone used by God to share the Good News).
> "and _____ _____ in the Lord" (someone who belongs to and obeys Christ).

Verse 8 says that Tychicus was going to share news about Paul, and doing so would encourage the Colossians' hearts.

> How do news and testimonies from other believers help strengthen and encourage your heart as well? What news or story has done that recently?

colossians

Onesimus

Much of what we know about Onesimus we learn from Paul's letter to a man named Philemon. It just so happened that Philemon was Onesimus' master. Onesimus was a native of Colossae but had fled servanthood to hide in Rome. Many scholars suggest that he also stole some of his master's money or property, making him a wanted fugitive. While he was running, Onesimus met Paul, but more importantly, he came to know Jesus. We see in the letter to Philemon that becoming a Christian radically changed Onesimus' life.

The Bible's book of Philemon is a short, one-chapter letter. Take a moment to read it. Jot down what you learn about Onesimus and his situation. Why was he headed back to Colossae?

In Colossians 4:9, Paul reminds the Church that Onesimus is *"one of you."* He was saying Onesimus was not just a fellow Colossian but a fellow Christian. Look at the terms used to describe him. Remember that Onesimus was a slave. Do you notice any term missing in this description that Paul had used to describe Tychicus? What might Paul be expressing here?

Tychicus, a veteran minister (and friend to Paul). Onesimus, a new convert (and slave to Philemon). Both were called *"brother"* (vv. 7, 9). Both were chosen to represent Paul. And most importantly, both were chosen to help spread the gospel of Christ.

What might this remind you about who God chooses to spread His Word? What might this remind you about your own qualifications to be used by God for Kingdom work?

Praying Colossians 4:7–9

TODAY, LET'S PRAY FOR OUR VETERAN MINISTERS WE KNOW BY NAME. PRAY THEY WOULD NOT BECOME DISCOURAGED OR BURNT OUT IN DOING THE HARD WORK OF MINISTRY. PRAY THEY WOULD ENDURE AND BE ENCOURAGED THEMSELVES, EVEN AS THEY ARE ENCOURAGING OTHERS. PRAY ALSO FOR NEW CONVERTS TO RISE TO THE WORK AHEAD. PRAY FOR ANYONE YOU KNOW BY NAME WHO IS NEW TO MINISTRY. PRAY THEY MIGHT HAVE COURAGE AND STRENGTH FOR THE JOURNEY AHEAD.

Colossians 4:10–14

THE CHURCH IS FILLED WITH INDIVIDUAL, UNIQUE PEOPLE WHO WORK TOGETHER FOR CHRIST.

Yesterday we talked about the two people charged with delivering this letter in person: Tychicus and Onesimus. Today we are going to look at the people who wished to send their own greetings to the church of Colossae. Throughout today's study, we'll take note of what makes each person unique, and hopefully we'll emerge with a deeper appreciation for each person who makes up the church.

Aristarchus

Colossians 4:10 starts with a greeting from Aristarchus. It says here that he was Paul's *"fellow prisoner."* We learn more about Aristarchus in the book of Acts.

What happened to Aristarchus in Ephesus according to Acts 19:29?

He is also listed among those who were with Paul in Greece in Acts 20:4. Look at the verse right above (Acts 20:3). What were they experiencing in Greece?

According to Acts 27:2, Aristarchus also accompanied Paul to Rome on a what?

This means Aristarchus also survived what, mentioned in Acts 27:18-20?

Aristarchus did not live an easy life. He faced trials and hardships at every turn. Yet he remained faithful — yes, faithful to Paul, but most importantly, to Christ. Can you think of anyone who fits this description in your life?

Mark
Mark, the cousin of Barnabas, has an interesting story as well. He came along for the first missionary journey that Paul and Barnabas went on together. However, something happened.

Read Acts 15:36-40. What had Mark done? What did this cause? Who sided with Mark?

Colossians 4:10 was written years after this divide took place. These words are an encouragement to anyone who has had a disagreement with someone else and that difference of opinion caused a divide. What appears to be Paul's attitude toward Mark now? What does this teach you?

Mark was someone who had made a mistake, no doubt about it. But he was also someone who was given a second chance and proved himself to be a faithful follower of Christ. Can you think of anyone who fits this description in your life?

Jesus/Justus

Jesus (which means "Joshua" in Hebrew) was a common name. This man Jesus, who is called Justus, is only mentioned here in this letter. We know nothing about him other than the fact that he was Jewish (a *"[man] of the circumcision"*) and that he was a comfort to Paul. (v. 11) He might not have made a big name for himself, but Justus looked for and used what they had in common (he and Paul were both Jewish Christians) and became a friend.

In what ways might we look around and find someone who needs a friend today? How can we be a comfort?

Epaphras

We learned in Colossians 1:7 that Epaphras was the one who first preached the gospel in Colossae. Scholars believe that Epaphras probably heard the gospel from Paul in Ephesus and then brought the Good News back to his hometown of Colossae and planted a church there.

First, let's look at Colossians 4:13. Here we learn that Epaphras also worked hard for what other two cities? (The first was just a few miles northwest of Colossae, and the second was 5 miles north of there.)

Now when we look back at Colossians 4:12, we see it mentions that Epaphras was always *"struggling on [their] behalf in his prayers..."* Here we have a picture of a praying leader with a heart for his surrounding community. In what ways can you better love, serve and pray for your local community?

Luke

Colossians 4:14 mentions *"Luke the beloved physician."* Luke was with Paul for much of his third missionary journey as well as looking in on him during several of his imprisonments. What a blessing it must have been to have a physical doctor nearby, especially considering the many beatings Paul received. Luke was also a gifted researcher and writer. We have him to thank for our New Testament books of Luke and Acts.

In Luke, we see someone who used his secular profession and talents to bless the Church in huge ways. Who do you know who also fits this description? How might you use your profession or talents for Jesus?

Demas
The last person mentioned who sent their greeting was a man named Demas. In Philemon 1:24, Demas was considered a *"fellow worker"* in Christ.

However, what happened later, according to 2 Timothy 4:10?

Sometimes there are those in the Church who, at one time, played a big part. However, for whatever reason, they walk away. Instead of being discouraged by this, let's be encouraged in knowing the Church will go on! How might the story of Demas encourage you to persevere even as we sadly watch some people walk away?

One final question for today. Look back over the names we studied today and how different each person was. What does this teach you about the Church?

Praying Colossians 4:10–14

PRAY FOR THE ARISTARCHUSES YOU KNOW — THOSE WHO ARE FACING HARDSHIPS AND TRIALS FOR JESUS. PRAY FOR THE MARKS — THOSE WHO HAVE MADE MISTAKES BUT ARE LOOKING FOR SECOND CHANCES. PRAY FOR THE JUSTUSES — THOSE WHO ARE QUIETLY COMFORTING AND BEING A FRIEND. PRAY FOR THE EPAPHRASES — THOSE WHO HAVE A HEART FOR THEIR COMMUNITIES. STOP AND PRAY FOR YOUR COMMUNITY AS WELL. PRAY FOR THE LUKES — THOSE PROFESSIONALS AND THOSE WITH TALENTS, THAT THEY WOULD STEP OUT TO BLESS OTHERS IN JESUS' NAME. PRAY FOR THE DEMASES — THAT THOSE WHO HAVE WALKED AWAY MIGHT FIND THEIR WAY BACK TO JESUS.

Colossians 4:15–18

THE CHURCH IS ONE BIG FAMILY.

Yesterday we looked at the many people who wanted to send their greetings and encouragement to their brothers and sisters in Colossae. Today, we'll look at Paul's own personal, final greetings as we close this letter.

Colossians 4:15 says, *"Give my greetings to the brothers at Laodicea..."* We mentioned yesterday that Laodicea was several miles (close to 10, some say) [1] to the west/northwest of Colossae.

> What does verse 16 mention should take place between the church of Colossae and that of Laodicea?

> What a beautiful example of fellowship and collaboration between two local churches. What does this remind us about the Church as a whole? Do you see this kind of fellowship and collaboration between local churches today? Why or why not?

Colossians 4:15 also says Paul sent his greetings *"to Nympha and the church in her house."* During this time, there were no buildings set aside specifically for Christian worship. People would simply gather in the home of a member who willingly offered their hospitality. Nympha opened her home to her church family in Laodicea. Let's see where other local churches gathered.

Read Philemon verses 1-2. Where did the church of Colossae meet?

Read Acts 16:40. This was while Paul was in Philippi. Where did the Philippian church meet?

Read Romans 16:23. We believe this to be a reference to the church in Corinth. Who hosted the church there?

Read 1 Corinthians 16:19. This is a reference to the church in Ephesus. Where did they meet?

What is a creative way you can open your own home to "be the Church"?

In Colossians 4:17, Paul singled out a man named Archippus. We do not know much about him, other than he is listed in Philemon verse 2. From there, it seems Archippus was part of Philemon's household, perhaps even his son. Or he could simply have been a member of the church gathered in Philemon's house. Either way, he is called out specifically. We do not know what this *"ministry"* is that he received from the Lord, but Paul wanted him to keep at it (v. 17)! And he wanted the church to encourage Archippus with those words as well.

Who can you specifically single out to encourage today? Who needs to hear the words "Keep at it!"?

In the final verse of this letter, we have the perfect wrap-up to our study. Letters were often dictated and then transcribed (this letter was probably transcribed by Timothy, as he is mentioned in Colossians 1:1). But here at the end, Paul takes the pen himself and uses his own handwriting to sign off on the letter. This had two purposes. First, it showed **affection.**

In our day and age of typing, emailing and texting, what effect might a handwritten note still have? When was the last time you wrote or received something handwritten?

The second purpose of Paul signing the letter himself was **authentication**. Remember how we have mentioned the danger of false teachers, especially in Colossae? The Church couldn't risk false doctrine. The Apostle Paul's letters carried authority and were divinely inspired. The Church needed to know the source of their teachings was accurate and true.

As we end this study that has focused so much attention on the world of divided opinions (especially brought in by false teachers) ... take a moment to read 1 Timothy 6:3-5 and jot down your thoughts as they relate to our study.

Knowing Truth is so important. Once more, according to John 14:6, where do we find Truth?

Friend, I pray that there would only be one source of Truth for you. Only Jesus. I pray that the world, with all its divided opinions and loud voices, would be silenced in your soul and that the peace of His Word would stand firm in your heart and mind.

Praying Colossians 4:15–18

AS WE PRAY THE FINAL VERSES OF COLOSSIANS, PRAY FOR YOUR BROTHERS AND SISTERS IN OTHER LOCAL CHURCHES AND OTHER DENOMINATIONS. PRAY FOR UNITY IN THE CHURCH. PRAY FOR OUR HOMES TO BECOME PLACES OF WORSHIP AND TEACHING AND ENCOURAGEMENT. PRAY BY NAME FOR SOMEONE WHO NEEDS ENCOURAGEMENT TODAY. AND FINALLY, PRAY THAT THE LORD WOULD HELP YOU KNOW THE TRUTH, RECOGNIZE THE TRUTH AND ACT UPON THE TRUTH. IN JESUS' NAME, AMEN AND AMEN.

Weekend Reflections

Welcome to our final weekend. We're looking at divided opinions and how we can know the Truth through God's Word.

This week, we studied many names in this letter's final greeting. And while on the surface these might just look like names of people we don't know, these names teach us something important about the Church.

For Week 5, read the section titled **"My Personal Relationship With Jesus vs. My Relationship With the Church"** on page 142.

Have you witnessed division in terms of more emphasis on either individual spirituality or community? Where specifically?

What do you learn about the truth from God's Word?

How can you walk in the Truth this week?

My Personal Relationship With Jesus vs. My Relationship With the Church

On our final look at dividing opinions, we are going to examine two different relationships we have as Christians. On one side, we have our personal relationship with Jesus. This is individualistic — just me and God. On the other side, we have our relationship with the Church. This is community. Sometimes Christians lean toward one side being more important than the other. Let's see what the Bible has to say.

My Personal Relationship With Jesus

Each of us who call ourselves Christ-followers received a personal invitation for salvation. This was an intimate and individual moment for each of us. And that personal relationship with God is absolutely vital. Jesus Himself demonstrated the need for alone time with His Father. (Mark 1:35; Luke 5:16) In fact, Jesus teaches us to get away privately and pray in secret. (Matthew 6:6) We need that one-on-one time with the Lord to strengthen our hearts, minds and souls.

The problem that sometimes arises is that our relationship with Jesus becomes so private we can forget that Jesus is not just a "Head" but an entire body. We say things like "Jesus is the only friend I need," but are we really just using that as an excuse not to love the body of Christ? Professor of Biblical Studies Howard Macy calls it "the self-interested isolation of private lives." [1] Interesting. Even our spiritual lives can become selfish if we are not careful.

My Relationship With the Church

There is much biblical evidence that the Christian life was intended to be lived in community. Hebrews 10:24-25 says we are to *stir up one another* and *not [neglect] to meet together, as is the habit of some..."* The first church in Acts was noted for its members' work as a community. (Acts 2:42-47) Jesus Himself said that where two or three people are gathered in His name, *"there am I among them"* (Matthew 18:20).

But honestly, community can be hard. The Church is made of imperfect people who can hurt us. Sometimes it feels safer to keep a distance. There are others who love the social aspects of the Church but want to keep it light and fun and impersonal. This is what Macy calls "the superficial social contacts that pass for 'Christian fellowship.'" [2]

What does this mean for us?

Romans 12:5 sums it up so well. It says, *"so we, though many, are one body in Christ, and individually members one of another."* We are individuals, with unique stories, gifts, situations and settings. We each have a personal relationship with Jesus that we nurture and grow, in the quiet, private moments of our lives. But we are also one body. We join together with those God loves, creating deep and meaningful relationships. Our personal relationship with Jesus will feed our relationships with others. And our relationships with others will help grow and feed our relationship with Jesus. This is not an either/or situation. This is both. God designed us to need both.

In Case You Were Wondering

Sometimes there is more to understanding Scripture than originally meets the eye. That's why our team wanted to provide you with additional information on some of the most popular verses from Colossians.

———

"And so, from the day we heard, we have not ceased to pray for you, asking that you may be filled with the knowledge of his will in all spiritual wisdom and understanding, so as to walk in a manner worthy of the Lord, fully pleasing to him: bearing fruit in every good work and increasing in the knowledge of God;"

MARISSA HENLEY

In this prayer for the church in Colossae, Paul prayed for both the cause and the effect in their spiritual lives. Paul understood that their beliefs would drive their behavior. If they fell prey to the false teaching that threatened the church at Colossae, they would not bear fruit for the Lord. In order to live out their Christian faith, they needed God to fill them with spiritual wisdom and understanding.

It's important to note that Paul isn't praying that they would walk in a worthy manner and please the Lord so that they would be saved. When he said, *"from the day we heard,"* he was referring to hearing about their faith in Christ Jesus (Colossians 1:9). It's clear from the previous verses that the Colossians had heard and accepted the gospel. Paul prayed that they would conduct themselves in a way that rightly reflected their status as God's redeemed children as they received His wisdom.

———

"He is the image of the invisible God, the firstborn of all creation. For by him all things were created, in heaven and on earth, visible and invisible, whether thrones or dominions or rulers or authorities—all things were created through him and for him."

MARISSA HENLEY

In these verses, Paul explained more about the Son in whom we have redemption. (Colossians 1:13-14) In the Son, the invisible God took on flesh, dwelt among us and showed us His glory. (John 1:14)

When Paul said the Son is *the firstborn of all creation*, he didn't mean that the Son was created first (v. 15). We know from elsewhere in Scripture that the Son wasn't created, but rather He has always been with the Father. (John 1:1-3)

Paul went on to say that all things were created by the Son, through the Son and for the Son. (Colossians 1:16)

"The firstborn of all creation" simply means that Christ ranks above all other beings (v. 15). Paul gave this extensive list of *"all things"* that were created by the Son to demonstrate the Son's preeminence over all of creation. All things were created by Him and for His glory.

———

"Therefore, as you received Christ Jesus the Lord, so walk in him, rooted and built up in him and established in the faith, just as you were taught, abounding in thanksgiving."

GRACE FOX

Placing our trust in Jesus for salvation marks the start of our Christian life. But God desires more for us than to just wear the label "Christian" and be content knowing heaven awaits when we take our last breath. He wants us to become vibrant, mature disciples of Christ who are committed to walking in step with His commands, not from a sense of religious duty but from love for Him and respect for His rightful authority over us. (John 14:15, 21)

He wants our roots to go deep into Christ's teachings and person so the winds of cultural change and life's storms cannot topple us. (Ephesians 3:17; Jeremiah 17:7-8) He wants us to continually grow stronger in our understanding of His Truth through the study of His Word. (2 Timothy 2:15) And He wants us to overflow with gratitude for what Christ has done for us.

"See to it that no one takes you captive by philosophy and empty deceit, according to human tradition, according to the elemental spirits of the world, and not according to Christ. For in him the whole fullness of deity dwells bodily,"

MARY BOSWELL

In Colossians 2, Paul reminded the Colossians of their faith and understanding through Christ, warning of deceit from false teachers that led to wisdom focused on humanity instead of Christ. When focused on Christ and His knowledge and authority through God, the Colossians would experience His absolute deity as fully man and fully God. (John 1:1-2; Colossians 1:19-20; Hebrews 2:17)

Just as Paul warned the Colossians, we, too, must guard against the dangers of deception from false teaching that leads us to shift our focus from Christ to this world. With the armor of God's Word, we navigate arguments and test spirits that set themselves up in the world against Christ, and we conquer the lies of the enemy. (2 Corinthians 10:5; 1 John 4:1-3) Upon that defeat and our acknowledgment of Christ as the Son of God, we understand the power of God through His Word and Truth found in Christ. (1 John 4:15)

"If then you have been raised with Christ, seek the things that are above, where Christ is, seated at the right hand of God. Set your minds on things that are above, not on things that are on earth."

KIMBERLY HENDERSON

Although our feet still presently walk the dusty roads of this Earth, we as believers have already been positionally "raised" with Christ. Paul tells us in Colossians 2:12 that we have been *"raised with [Christ] through faith."* Ephesians 2:5-6 goes on to say that because we have been saved by faith, we have been raised with Christ and seated in the heavenly places. Now, in Colossians 3:1-2, Paul reminds us we are to seek and set our minds on things that are above. The Greek word used for "seek" in Colossians 3:1 means to "look for; desire." Because we have experienced a change in position, there should also be a change in our pursuits and passions. Our longings should shift from that which is temporal to all that is eternal. And since we pursue what we desire, we should now be found pursuing Jesus — looking to Him, learning from Him, leaning into Him and leading others to Him.

"Put to death therefore what is earthly in you:
sexual immorality, impurity, passion, evil desire,
and covetousness, which is idolatry."

KAREN EHMAN

The actions mentioned in this list are all forms of the final one mentioned: idolatry. Idolatry is defined as anything that takes the rightful place of God in our lives. When we succumb to a lust such as sexual immorality or covetousness, we are placing ourselves and our passions above God and His desires for us. This passage declares that we are to *"put to death"* such actions (v. 5). This concept doesn't merely mean to practice self-discipline. The original Greek word used means "to render weak or impotent; to murder or kill." The Christian is commanded to kill any self-centeredness, shifting focus from self to God. Anything that keeps us from fully obeying and surrendering to Jesus Christ must be spiritually exterminated. Jesus Himself taught this in Matthew 5:29-30.

———

"Put on then, as God's chosen ones, holy and beloved, compassionate hearts, kindness, humility, meekness, and patience,"

SARAH FRAZER

In the original Greek, the word for "elected" simply means chosen, and it refers to those who have placed their faith in Christ. Many passages in the Bible refer to believers as "chosen." (Matthew 20:15; Romans 8:33; 2 Timothy 2:10) The point of Colossians 3:12 isn't to debate election versus free will of man.

Paul brings up election to encourage believers to walk with mercy, kindness, humbleness and kindness. It is to remind us that because we are chosen — set apart — by a loving and holy God, we, too, are called to live lives reflecting Him.

colossians

———

"bearing with one another and, if one has a complaint against another, forgiving each other; as the Lord has forgiven you, so you also must forgive."

JOY A. WILLIAMS

Reading the words *"bearing with one another"* may feel like a requirement to put up with someone else's faults and failures in our own strength. However, "bear" is the Greek word *"anechō,"* which can also mean for us to "hold [ourselves] back or up." But our restraint is not based on our own strength. The grace we've been given by Christ enables us to respond to others like Christ would respond.

By God's grace, my sins are forgiven. But His forgiveness doesn't just give us relief. It also gives us the reason to "hold ourselves back"

from bitterness and resentment for the sin of others. Our complaint against someone may be justifiable. There may be ethical and legal ways to hold them accountable. But unforgiveness is unbiblical.

As we "hold ourselves up" to the holy standard of forgiveness, we see forgiveness is not based on our emotions; it is tied to God's compassion. So we *"also must forgive."* Otherwise, we remain tethered to someone else's offense. Thankfully, Jesus died for their sin on the cross — while also dying for ours.

colossians

"Wives, submit to your husbands,
as is fitting in the Lord."

BRONWYN CARDWELL

God created and established the family as a picture of His relationship to those He created in His image. The husband represents Christ, who loved His bride, the Church, so much that He died in order to save her. The Church represents the wife, who should yield to and reverence her husband with a willing spirit. The husband is told to give up his life for his wife as Christ did for the Church. (Ephesians 5:25) As part of His perfect design, wives are told to *"submit to [their] husbands, as is fitting in the Lord."* Paul expresses this same thought in Ephesians 5:21. The word "submit" in Greek is the same word used to express mankind's duty to governing powers, which is evidenced through subjection and reverence. In the bonds of marriage, wives are not submitting to a disinterested authority but to their own husbands, who are to love them with tender and faithful affection, (Colossians 3:19) *"just as Christ loved the church and gave Himself for her"* (Ephesians 5:25). Following God's blueprint for marriage is an example to the watching world of God's perfect design and His loving heart for His creation.

———

"Whatever you do,
work heartily,
as for the Lord
and not for men,"

CHRISTINA PATTERSON

The book of Colossians highlights the unique deity of Jesus Christ to combat false teachings circulating at the time. The author of Colossians, however, does not only want to encourage his readers to believe the Truth about Jesus but to live the Truth in their everyday lives. Wisdom is given on how to conduct ourselves as those with new life in Christ. The letter instructs us that our belief in God should be reflected in our work for God, whether it's our parenting, marriage or career. The letter does not serve as a simple checklist on what to do but as inspiration on why we should behave the way God has called us. We are reminded that whatever we do, we are not working for man but God. Therefore, the excellence of our work should be a reflection of the truly finished work of Christ.

End
Notes

Letter to Colossians: The Recipient
[1] Barton, B., Comfort, P., Osborne, G., Taylor, L.K., Veerman, D. *Life Application New Testament Commentary.* Wheaton, IL: Tyndale House Publishers, Inc., 2001. pp.867.

Day 2
[1] Swindoll, Charles R. *Swindoll's Living Insights New Testament Commentary: Philippians, Colossians, Philemon.* Carol Stream, IL: Tyndale House Publishers, Inc., 2017. pp. 115.

Day 3
[1] Wright, N.T. *Colossians and Philemon.* Tyndale New Testament Commentaries, vol. 12. Downers Grove, IL: InterVarsity Press, USA, 1986. pp. 56.

[2] Gorday, Peter J., editor. *Ancient Christian Commentary on Scripture: New Testament, vol IX.,* general editor Thomas C. Oden. Downers Grove, IL: InterVarsity Press, 2000. pp. 4.

Day 4
[1] Henry, M. *Matthew Henry's commentary on the whole Bible: complete and unabridged in one volume.* Peabody: Hendrickson, 1994. pp. 2330.

Day 5
[1] Wright, N.T. *Colossians and Philemon.* Tyndale New Testament Commentaries, vol. 12. Downers Grove, IL: InterVarsity Press, USA, 1986. pp. 62.

[2] Thompson, Jeremy. *Bible Sense Lexicon: Dataset Documentation.* Bellingham, WA: Faithlife, 2015.

Truth vs. Grace
[1] DeYoung, Kevin. "Full of Grace and Truth." *The Gospel Coalition,* 3 June 2014, https://www.thegospelcoalition.org/blogs/kevin-deyoung/full-of-grace-and-truth/. Accessed February 2021.

Hymns in the New Testament
[1] Pliny, *Lib.* 10.96.7. Translation from Betty Radice, *Pliny: Letters and Panegyrics,* vol. 2, *Letters VIII-X,* Loeb Classical Library, ed. G. P. Goold, vol. 59. Cambridge, MA: Harvard University Press, 1969.

[2] Swindoll, Charles R. *Swindoll's Living Insights New Testament Commentary: Philippians, Colossians, Philemon.* Carol Stream, IL: Tyndale House Publishers, Inc., 2017. pp. 124.

Day 8
[1] Barton, B., Comfort, P., Osborne, G., Taylor, L.K., Veerman, D. *Life Application New Testament Commentary.* Wheaton, IL: Tyndale House Publishers, Inc., 2001. pp. 875.

Day 9
[1] Wright, N.T. *Colossians and Philemon.* Tyndale New Testament Commentaries, vol. 12. Downers Grove, IL: InterVarsity Press, USA, 1986. pp. 94.

Day 10
[1] Thompson, Jeremy. *Bible Sense Lexicon: Dataset Documentation.* Bellingham, WA: Faithlife, 2015.

[2] Henry, M. *Matthew Henry's commentary on the whole Bible: complete and unabridged in one volume.* Peabody: Hendrickson, 1994. pp. 2332.

Condemnation vs. Conviction
[1] Ballenger, Mark. "What is the Difference Between Condemnation and Conviction?" *Apply God's Word,* 7 August 2017, https://applygodsword.com/what-is-the-difference-between-condemnation-and-conviction/. Accessed February 2021.

colossians

Day 14

[1] Wright, N.T. *Colossians and Philemon*. Tyndale New Testament Commentaries, vol. 12. Downers Grove, IL: InterVarsity Press, USA, 1986. pp. 123-124.

[2] *The ESV Study Bible*. Wheaton, IL: Crossway, 2008. pp. 2290.

Worldly Wisdom vs. Spiritual Wisdom

[1] Wilkin, Jen. "Why It's So Important to Know the Difference Between 'Godly' and 'Worldly' Wisdom." *Relevant Magazine,* Relevant Media Group, Inc., 31 July 2018, www.relevantmagazine.com/faith/why-its-so-important-to-know-the-difference-between-godly-and-worldly-wisdom/. Accessed February 2021.

Day 16

[1] Swanson, J. *Dictionary of Biblical Languages with Semantic Domains: Greek (New Testament)* (electronic ed.). Oak Harbor: Logos Research Systems, Inc., 1997.

[2] Soeiro, Loren. "Why Are Millennials So Anxious And Unhappy?" *Psychology Today.* https://www.psychologytoday.com/us/blog/i-hear-you/201907/why-are-millennials-so-anxious-and-unhappy. Accessed January 2021.

[3] Mcmaster, Geoff. "Millennials and Gen Z are more anxious than previous generations: here's why." *University of Alberta.* https://www.ualberta.ca/folio/2020/01/millennials-and-gen-z-are-more-anxious-than-previous-generations-heres-why.html. Accessed January 2021.

Day 17

[1] Wright, N.T. *Colossians and Philemon*. Tyndale New Testament Commentaries, vol. 12. Downers Grove, IL: InterVarsity Press, USA, 1986. pp. 138.

[2] Swanson, J. (1997). *Dictionary of Biblical Languages with Semantic Domains: Greek (New Testament)* (electronic ed.). Oak Harbor: Logos Research Systems, Inc.

[3] Wright, N.T. *Colossians and Philemon*. Tyndale New Testament Commentaries, vol. 12. Downers Grove, IL: InterVarsity Press, USA, 1986. pp. 139.

Day 18

[1] Barton, B., Comfort, P., Osborne, G., Taylor, L.K., Veerman, D. *Life Application New Testament Commentary*. Wheaton, IL: Tyndale House Publishers, Inc., 2001. pp. 884.

Day 19

[1] Liddell, H. G., Scott, R., Jones, H. S., & McKenzie, R. (1996). *A Greek-English lexicon* (p. 571). Oxford: Clarendon Press.

[2] Moo, Douglas. *Letters to the Colossians and to Philemon*. Grand Rapids, MI: Wm. B. Eerdmans Publishing Co., 2008. pp. 290.

Day 20

[1] Lewis, C.S. "The Sermon and the Lunch." *Undeceptions: Essays on Theology and Ethics,* edited by Walter Hooper. London: Geoffrey Bles., 1971. pp. 237.

[2] Wright, N.T. *Colossians and Philemon*. Tyndale New Testament Commentaries, vol. 12. Downers Grove, IL: InterVarsity Press, USA, 1986. pp. 152-153.

[3] Ibid.

Humility, Meekness, Submission and Servanthood vs. Modern Society
[1] Carter, Paul. "3 Things Biblical Humility Is (And Isn't) - The Gospel Coalition: Canada." *The Gospel Coalition | Canada,* 31 May 2020, ca.thegospelcoalition.org/columns/ad-fontes/3-things-biblical-humility-is-and-isnt/. Accessed February 2021.

[2] "Meekness Synonyms, Meekness Antonyms." *Merriam-Webster,* Merriam-Webster, www.merriam-webster.com/thesaurus/meekness. Accessed February 2021.

[3] "Meekness." *Dictionary.com,* Dictionary.com, www.dictionary.com/browse/meekness?s=t. Accessed February 2021.

[4] Caner, Mark E. "Spiritual Meekness: An Imperative Virtue for Christian Leaders." *Inner Resources for Leaders, School of Global Leadership & Entrepreneurship,* Regent University. www.regent.edu/acad/global/publications/innerresources/vol2iss3/caner.pdf. Accessed February 2021.

[5] *The ESV Study Bible.* Wheaton, IL: Crossway, 2008. pp. 1828.

[6] Piper, John. "Six Things Submission Is Not." *Desiring God,* 18 Feb. 2021, www.desiringgod.org/articles/six-things-submission-is-not. Accessed February 2021.

[7] Archer, Brad. "Seven Marks of a Godly Servant." *Unlocking the Bible,* 22 Mar. 2019, unlockingthebible.org/2016/05/seven-marks-of-a-godly-servant/. Accessed February 2021.

Day 21
[1] Swindoll, Charles R. *Swindoll's Living Insights New Testament Commentary: Philippians, Colossians, Philemon.* Carol Stream, IL: Tyndale House Publishers, Inc., 2017. pp. 182.

[2] Ibid.

[3] *The ESV Study Bible.* Wheaton, IL: Crossway, 2008. pp. 2299.

Day 22
[1] Swindoll, Charles R. *Swindoll's Living Insights New Testament Commentary: Philippians, Colossians, Philemon.* Carol Stream, IL: Tyndale House Publishers, Inc., 2017. pp. 187.

[2] Barclay, William. *Letters to the Philippians, Colossians, and Thessalonians.* Louisville, KY: Westminster John Knox Press, 2019. pp. 195.

Day 25
[1] Barton, B., Comfort, P., Osborne, G., Taylor, L.K., Veerman, D. *Life Application New Testament Commentary.* Wheaton, IL: Tyndale House Publishers, Inc., 2001. pp. 889.

My Personal Relationship With Jesus vs. My Relationship With the Church
[1] Macy, Howard. "Community: God's Design For Growth." *Bible.org,* 29 May 2011, bible.org/article/community-god%E2%80%99s-design-growth. Accessed February 2021.

[2] Ibid.

colossians

DO YOU WANT TO KNOW AND LIVE THE TRUTH OF GOD'S WORD, BUT NEED DAILY REMINDERS TO HELP YOU?

Encouragement for Today devotions are free daily devotions sent straight to your inbox.

GO TO PROVERBS31.ORG/READ/DEVOTIONS TO SIGN UP FOR FREE!

Want to listen to biblical teaching from Proverbs 31 Ministries while you're getting ready in the morning, driving to work or running errands?

CHECK OUT THE PROVERBS 31 MINISTRIES PODCAST

Subscribe on iTunes today!

About
Proverbs 31
Ministries

She is clothed with strength and dignity;
she can laugh at the days to come.

PROVERBS 31:25

Proverbs 31 Ministries is a nondenominational, nonprofit Christian ministry that seeks to lead women into a personal relationship with Christ. With Proverbs 31:10-31 as a guide, Proverbs 31 Ministries reaches women in the middle of their busy days through free devotions, podcast episodes, speaking events, conferences, resources, online Bible studies and training in the call to write, speak and lead others.

We are real women offering real-life solutions to those striving to maintain life's balance, in spite of today's hectic pace and cultural pull away from godly principles.

Wherever a woman may be on her spiritual journey, Proverbs 31 Ministries exists to be a trusted friend who understands the challenges she faces and walks by her side, encouraging her as she walks toward the heart of God.

Visit us online today at proverbs31.org!

Proverbs 31
MINISTRIES